FIGURE SKATING

FIGURE

NEW YORK   1978   ATHENEUM

SKATING

Dianne DeLeeuw

WITH STEVE LEHRMAN

Library of Congress Cataloging in Publication Data
DeLeeuw, Dianne.
  Figure Skating.
  Bibliography: p.
  1. Skating. I. Lehrman, Steve. II. Title.
GV850.4.D44 1978   796.9′1   77-76798
ISBN 0-689-10820-6

The authors wish to thank the following organizations for their cooperation in compiling photographic material for this volume:

Holiday On Ice

Madison Square Garden, New York

Corona & Liebenow Skate Shops, New York

Riedell Shoes, Inc., Red Wing, Minnesota

Lubin's Rink & Bowling Supply, Watertown, Massachusetts

Instructional Photographs of Ms. DeLeeuw by Michael Lipack

Diagrams by Myron Ronis

Contents

FIGURE SKATING

Introduction

SKATING HAS been a part of me as long as I can remember. I can't imagine a time when I wasn't on skates.

My mother was born and raised in Holland, where she learned to skate on the frozen canal in front of her house. In the winter she would get together with her friends and spend hours skating and having fun.

When my mother came to the United States she hoped to be able to continue skating and was pleasantly surprised to find she did not even have to wait for freezing weather. Now she could skate year round on the artificial ice at indoor rinks. She joined a skating club and in no time at all had passed her preliminary figure skating achievement test.

When I was very young I accompanied my mom to the

rink where she would join a group of women to skate for exercise and recreation.

As the women traveled around the ice, I banded together with the other children to create as much mischief and make as much noise as possible. Our mothers finally decided that the only solution was to give us skates and rope off a small portion of the rink for our use. Little did my mother know what she was getting herself into. Instead of hanging on to the railing like the rest of the kids, I skated over every inch of the area. When it came time to go home, I screamed and cried. At four years of age I was hooked on skating.

It wasn't long before the trips to the rink were for my lessons, not my mother's.

One of the retired men at the rink taught me different ice games, which further increased my love of skating.

I watched the older kids doing their figures and other beautiful maneuvers on the ice. I tried to copy them on my own, and it soon became evident I was ready for formal figure skating lessons.

Finding a good teacher was easy. I skated at Paramount Skating Rink in Paramount, California. The rink is owned by Frank Zamboni, inventor of the popular Zamboni Ice Resurfacing Machine. This was the home of the Arctic Blades Figure Skating Club, one of the top competitive organizations in the United States.

At the age of six I passed my preliminary test and was on my way.

I skated in competitions and continued taking skating

achievement tests. I wanted to complete the tests as quickly as possible so I could reach the Senior Lady Classification while I still was young.

My life was a busy one. I was at the rink for two hours of skating before school, and I headed right back to the rink as soon as classes were over. Even with my full schedule I graduated from high school, with honors, at the age of sixteen.

By 1971 I had passed my final figure test (the gold medal) and decided to enter high-level competition. I took advantage of my dual United States-Holland citizenship (my mother was a Dutch citizen) and left California to compete in the National Championships in Holland.

The decision to leave home was a difficult one. I didn't know a soul in Holland and had only spoken Dutch with my family, never in public. But everything worked out well and I suddenly found myself the National Champion of the Netherlands. I went on to represent them in the European Championships.

My dream of being in international competition had come true. It was 1972 and I set my sights on making the Olympic team.

It was quite a thrill to travel to Japan as a member of the Dutch Olympic team. I placed sixteenth in the competition, but that didn't matter. Just being a part of the 1972 Olympics is something I will always treasure.

Now that I had a taste of the Olympics, my goal was clear. I wanted to win a medal at the 1976 Olympic

Games at Innsbruck, Austria.

I spent the next year training as hard as I could for the competitions. But at the 1973 World Championships a poor performance resulted in a fifteenth-place finish.

My first reaction was to forget my dream. For a while I really thought about quitting competitive skating. Instead, I changed my attitude and once again decided to put all my effort and energy into skating. By the next autumn it all paid off.

In October I skated in England for the Richmond Trophy. This was the first major international ladies' competition of the season. I didn't have a lot of confidence as I took to the ice, but after two days of competition I was holding the famous Richmond Trophy!

The rest of the season was quite a thrill. I won second place in the 1974 European Championships in Zagreb, Yugoslavia. Then I captured a bronze medal in the World Championships in Munich behind Christine Errath of East Germany and Dorothy Hamill of the United States. No one believed that after a fifteenth-place finish I could come back and win a bronze medal. In the world of figure skating that great a turnaround is very rare. But it happened, and I was very happy.

I put in a lot of unbelievably hard work in preparation for the next year's contests. By the time we began to compete, I was ready.

I won my fifth National title and missed first place in the European Championships by one one-hundredth of a point!

The next competition was the World Championships at Colorado Springs, Colorado. I knew the high altitude and thin air could present a problem, so I arrived early and worked myself into top physical shape. As luck would have it, I managed to catch strep throat. Practice became difficult, sometimes impossible.

Fortunately, I was still able to perform well. By the time the compulsories were over I had such a large lead that I would have had to give a horrendous free skating program to lose. I didn't. In fact, I won the free skating competition with a clean sweep of first-place votes from the judges and became the World Figure Skating Champion of 1975.

The next year was a hectic one. I combined exhibitions and personal appearances with a great deal of hard training. I also took ballet lessons three times a week to get into perfect condition. By the end of the summer I was skating better than at any time in my life. I was eagerly awaiting the Olympic Games.

Then disaster struck. I arrived home in California after a whirlwind tour of television appearances in Europe, ready to polish my routines. One Monday I was preparing to give an exhibition of my new program. I was warming up and jumped into a double axel. The takeoff was fine, but as I went to land my free leg wouldn't move. When I landed I felt an excruciating pain as something tore in my left hip.

I limped off the ice, still determined to return and perform my routine. But there was no way I could skate.

I couldn't move my leg from front to back without terrible pain.

I went to several doctors. All had the same opinion: "Take a month or two off, rest, and let the leg heal." "Before the Olympics!" was my standard, outraged reply. I could see all my hard work and years of effort going down the drain. I finally found a physical therapist and doctor who treated me with electrical currents, ultrasound, and other devices I never knew existed.

For a month my work on the ice was confined to simple strokes to keep up my stamina and compulsory figures (figure eights). I had to put it all together in time for the National Championships in Holland.

And put it together I did! I received a perfect score of 6.0 in the free skating and went on to win the long elusive European Championship. I was named Sportswoman of the Year.

All that was left was the Olympics.

The 1976 games were an exciting, tension-filled two weeks. When they were over I headed home with a silver medal—and a difficult decision to make.

In my heart I knew I wanted to continue skating. But to spend another year in hard training was too much.

Joining an ice show seemed to be the answer. I could still enjoy skating as well as entertain people. I signed a contract with Holiday on Ice and Ice Follies that May. By June I was rehearsing for my first professional engagement.

I now had to make the transition from competitive

skater to show performer. As a competitor I practiced every day in preparation for a few major championships. Now I am on the ice performing sometimes two and three shows a day. Before I was working toward perfection in a meet, now I have to be at my best every time I take to the ice. Much to my surprise, it didn't take long to make this adjustment.

Skating with a show has been very fulfilling. In this day and age it is a wonderful feeling to know that I can take people away from their cares and worries into a fantasy land of beautiful skating.

In this book I hope to give you my knowledge, skills, and some of my love for skating. So, on with the book and happy skating!

History of Skating

SKATING IS one of the oldest methods of transportation known to man. Bone skates, dating as far back as 2000 B.C., have been unearthed in England and Northern Europe. Men were able to glide along the ice with the bone strapped to their footwear. Bone skates had no edges, so the skater had to propel himself and steer by using poles held in each hand.

The early literature of Scandinavia and Iceland includes references to ice skating. Mention is made of the iron skate at about the time iron was becoming a widely used material (circa eighth century B.C.).

These iron "skates" did not actually have blades. They were wide straps attached to wooden blocks. This assembly was fastened to the footwear.

Most historians agree that the first bladed skate originated in the Netherlands. The bladed skate had edges. Blade edges were used to push and steer on the ice. Poles were eliminated, and the skater's hands and arms were free. The Dutch discovered a natural method of stroking by using their edges.

Frigid weather conditions in the Netherlands froze canals and provided long expanses of ice surface. The canals were used as transportation and communication links between villages.

Although we cannot date precisely when skating became popular, it must have been prior to 1498. A wood engraving with this date depicts a scene in which a girl wearing bladed skates has fallen on the ice. Other skaters in the picture appear to be stroking in a manner similar to today.

Early skaters took to the ice because it was practical transportation, but it wasn't long before skating also became a leisure time activity.

The edges of bladed skates made it possible to travel at higher velocities, and soon skaters were competing against each other in speed contests. Racing became popular, and by the sixteenth century speed skating was a well organized sport. Nowadays when a speed skating competition takes place, skaters from Holland perennially dominate the field.

By the mid-seventeenth century a great portion of Holland's population were recreational skaters. When the aristocracy took to the ice, they shunned speed skating. They were more interested in creating an elegant skating style. This stylish skating proved to be the birth of figure skating.

The English, however, contributed more to the style and creativity of figure skating than did the Dutch. Skating in England began as a recreational activity. There were no frozen canals, no long distances to travel. Ponds and lakes were the skating sites of England.

It did not take long for the English to realize that the low, flat skate so perfect for traveling on the long Netherland canals would not do on the smaller skating surfaces in England. This skate was not made for the constant turns and circles that had to be negotiated on the English ponds. So, in the early eighteenth century the English created the first figure skate.

This skate blade was short and curved in the front, which facilitated turning. It is a tribute to the English that to this day most quality figure skating blades are manufactured in the United Kingdom.

The first figure skaters became quite involved with the new sport. All their time on the ice was spent tracing figures in the frozen surface. As their abilites increased, and competitions began, figures of increased complexity were developed. Everything from the letters of the alphabet to ornate filigree designs were etched into the ice.

Figure skating began to expand. While the English remained interested in the technique and science of the sport, in Paris figure skaters began to concentrate on elegance of style and beauty of movement.

Skating clubs were formed all over the world. The first

was organized in Edinburgh, Scotland, in 1742. It was not until 1849 that the United States had its first club, based in Philadelphia, Pennsylvania.

The International Skating Union (I.S.U.) was formed in 1892. The first international amateur skating competition took place in 1896. In the early competitions men and women skated against each other. In 1906 separate events were held for males and females.

The modern concept of figure skating was created by an American, Jackson Haines (1840–1875). Haines had been trained in ballet since childhood. He was a multitalented person, who worked as teacher of physical culture, juggler, exhibition skater, skating instructor, and ballet master.

Jackson had still another skill. As an inventor he developed an improved, safer skate. The blade clamped directly to the boot, providing greater strength than any previous model. It allowed skaters to move more athletically and increased jumping ability.

He envisioned skating as an art form, similar to dance. Haines transferred the drama and theatricality found in dance to the ice sport by implementing music and colorful costumes in his skating routines.

Haines's style of skating was certainly innovative. At first his new methods were rejected by skaters in America and England. The Austrians, however, understood and appreciated his theory of skating, and his pupils and followers in Austria began a ''Viennese School.'' It took some time, but gradually Haines's ideas gained acceptance throughout the skating world.

Next to Jackson Haines, I think that Sonja Henie had the greatest single impact on figure skating. In 1927, at the age of fourteen, she skated to the World Championship in her hometown of Oslo, Norway. The world saw a person very accomplished on skates, yet so young in years. Children now were encouraged to begin skating at very early ages.

During the late 1920s and 1930s Sonja's style was considered very athletic and vigorous. Her short skating skirts caused some controversy, but they were necessary to permit the freedom of movement essential to her skating style.

Sonja Henie was a ten-time World Champion and captured three Olympic gold medals (1928, 1932, 1936). This spectacular record created new international interest in the sport.

Once Sonja left the amateur ranks she made an even greater contribution to ice skating. As a professional skater she toured the United States with her ice review. Sonja culminated her career by appearing in a series of motion pictures that made figure skating known in every part of the world.

Ice skating presently falls into three categories: speed skating, figure skating, and hockey. All are Olympic events and are regulated by national and international associations.

Speed skating skills are relatively uncomplicated. Only a few basic skating strokes are used. Modern speed skating involves many scientific training programs. Skaters work to develop power, speed, and endurance. Perfecting the start is most important and exacting.

The speed skate has a long, flat, thin blade that provides a maximum amount of pushing surface and flow with a minimum of friction. The long blade can be dangerous when skating in close quarters, and many rinks prohibit speed skates at general sessions. Many rinks schedule special speed skating times, and interested skaters can join clubs to become more involved in the sport.

Speed skating became an Olympic event in 1924, for men only. It was not until 1960 that women competed for Olympic medals.

Olympic style speed skating on outdoor rinks is very popular in Europe, but there is only one such rink in the United States, in West Allis, Wisconsin.

The popularity of ice hockey has increased by leaps and bounds over the past ten years as both a spectator and participant sport. The game originated in Canada before the turn of the century and the first Olympic ice hockey tournament took place in 1920.

Any good hockey player must have a total mastery of basic strokes, stops, starts, and turns. In addition to skillful skating, players must be able to control a small puck with a hockey stick, and must be able to implement the strategy of the game.

Hockey blades stand between speed and figure blades in curvature and width. Balancing on these blades is more difficult, for they are higher and narrower with a sharp

15

A basic hockey skate. Note the rockered blade.

curvature at the front and back ends. The narrower blade creates less friction, making it easier for a skater to move quickly.

Figure skating is the most complex of the skating specialties. Athletic ability and skill are combined with artistic, musical, and choreographic elements. Much time is spent in rigorous training sessions. All basic strokes, edges, turns, jumps, spins, and figures must be mastered. Not to mention the precision needed for compulsory figures. A pairs skater also spends many hours perfecting lifts. Developing one's own characteristic skating style is another must for a figure skater.

The figure skating blade is wider, with more rocker— amount of curve in the radius of the blade—than the speed skate and less than a hockey skate. Faster and

Hockey and figure skates. Each is designed to permit maximum performance in its respective sport.

The serrated toe pick enables the figure skater to execute various jumps and spins.

easier turns and spins are possible. More of the blade can be used because a skater can balance farther forward or backward than on a hocky skate. The front of the blade has a set of picks (or teeth) that are used in jumps and spins.

There are three types of blades used by advanced figure skaters: (1) A blade with no master tooth to get in the way; it is ground with little or no hollow on the bottom of the blade for maximum flow. This is the blade used for compulsory figures. (2) A blade with a short heel. Used by some ice dancers to execute close, tricky steps. (3) A blade that is rockered with large toe picks for

17

toe jumps; it is very sharp with a deep hollow. This blade is used in free skating.

Figure skating made its debut in 1908 as an Olympic sport. Competitions are held for men and women in singles skating. They team up for the pairs skating and ice dancing contests.

Skating is a major source of entertainment all over the world. Ice shows are performed in nearly every town and city and are beamed by television to every part of the globe. Skaters who tour with these ice reviews are paid handsomely. The popularity of ice hockey fills arenas, making it possible for some players to earn over $100,000 in one season of play.

Crowds turn out to see the professionals, but the amateur skater still plays a large role in entertaining the public. Speed and figure skating competitions are held on regional, national, and international levels. The sellout crowds and large television audiences for these events testify that all skating sports are well received by the public on every level.

Equipment

MANY SPORTS require numerous pieces of equipment. Not so for skating. All you need is a pair of skates and you are ready to take to the ice. It is important to note that properly fitting skates are a major factor in your enjoyment and progress as a skater. The right skates will

Most quality figure skating boots and blades are purchased separately. They will be properly attached at the skate shop.

be a great asset. A poor fit will prove a distinct handicap.

The price of skates is usually in direct proportion to their quality.

If you are preparing to buy a pair of skates (or plan to rent them at a local rink), here are the four important factors to consider:

> Fit of Boot.
> Quality of Boot.
> Quality of Blade.
> Placement of Blade.

FIT OF BOOT

The boot should fit snugly over a thin sock. It should feel close, but not to the point of pinching. There should be enough room in front to allow the toes to wiggle, and the rear should be snug enough so the heel cannot raise up. Such a fit can provide maximum support.

Competitive skaters often order custom-made boots that mold to their feet. The boots may alleviate a foot problem, or simply provide greater comfort for those many hours spent on the ice.

Proper lacing of the skate boots will help supply maximum support and comfort.

When lacing the boot, make sure wrinkles don't form in the leather over the ankle bones. A gap of 1½ to 2 inches should separate the sides of the boot.

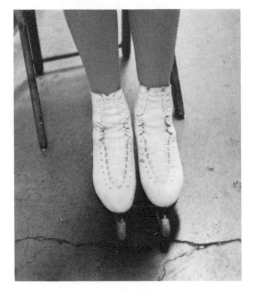

Properly laced boots will provide necessary support. Lace ends should always be tucked in the top of the boot.

Skates laced haphazardly (missed hooks, laces left loose, lace ends exposed) will make skating uncomfortable and dangerous.

The first few lower eyelets are to be laced loosely, permitting the toes to wiggle slightly.

The next section, over the ankle to just below the boot, must be firmly laced. This is the area that needs substantial support.

The remaining eyelets (or hooks) will be slightly looser than the midsection but still fairly firm. The amount of tightness is really up to your personal preference, but your boot should never be so loose as to fail to provide support.

Most boots will stretch with wear, so don't be afraid to purchase a tight-fitting boot. Then when your boots give, you can still maintain the support that is so necessary when skating. Keep in mind that skate boots usually run larger than street shoes. Your skate size will probably be one or two full sizes smaller than your everyday shoes.

QUALITY OF BOOT

The most important factor in boot quality is the amount of support built into the arch. A good boot will have a strong steel arch support (or counter) running from the heel forward to a point just behind the joint of the big toe. This support aides in keeping ankles straight so feet will not fall inward. So many beginners are discouraged because of "weak ankles." More often than not, their problem is caused by a boot not providing proper support.

Another point to consider is thickness of leather. The

hide should be sturdy and reasonably thick and firm.

If you are renting skates, it's a good idea to ask for the newest pair available in your size. Older skates are more likely to have stretched and softened leather, which may not provide the required support.

QUALITY OF BLADE

When purchasing blades, the higher the price, the better the quality of steel. A beginning skater does not have to be concerned with owning high-quality blades.

Attention should be paid to making sure the blades are properly sharpened. They should be "round honed." This means each blade is sharpened so it has two parallel edges running the length of the blade, with a rounded hollow between. Edges must be even and level. This is most important for the novice.

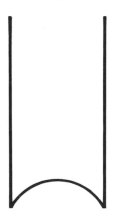

A round honed blade has two skating edges with a hollow between.

23

PLACEMENT OF BLADE

Blades should be mounted in a straight line that parallels the main axis of the boot. Some skaters like to have their blades set slightly inside of the axis line. The main factor is that the mounting is straight. The blade line and boot axis must *never* cross.

Some blades have slotted holes that enable the blade to be moved one-quarter inch after original mounting. Different people have different preferences, and these slots make it possible to reset the blades without drilling new holes in the boot.

Competitive skaters are often very picky about where the blade is set. For example, the moment I make my first stroke on a newly mounted pair of blades I can sense the slightest difference in placement over the old set.

CARE OF BLADES

To maintain your blades in good condition, keep these things in mind:

While wearing skates off the ice, never walk with exposed blades on anything but rubber, or, sparingly, on wood. Fortunately, most rinks are completely floored in rubber matting. Avoid cement floors, as they will dull your edges and can cause nicks and chips in the steel that

Blade guards are a worthwhile investment. They slip easily over the skate blades. The guards should be worn when walking to and from the ice. Use of these guards keep skates sharp, and prevents nicks in the steel.

could ruin the blade.

Invest in a pair of protective rubber or wooden blade guards. They slip over the blade and should be worn when walking to and from the ice.

Always dry blades with a chamois cloth or soft towel after skating.

Do not store skates with the guards on the blades. Moisture condensation will cause blades to rust. However, terry cloth can be quickly stitched together to make blade or boot covers that will protect the skates when not in use.

Check blades for any loose or missing screws.

A small tote bag should be used to carry your skates and other equipment.

These simple steps will keep your blades in good skating condition for a long time.

Clothing

FOR GENERAL SKATING there is one rule of thumb regarding clothing: it must be comfortable. For this reason, many skaters wear outfits made of stretch materials. Double-knit warm-up suits are comfortable and practical. They are easy to move in and provide warmth.

The amount of clothing depends on the temperature.

Indoor rinks are usually kept warm enough for wearing only a light jacket or sweater.

Outdoors, a windbreaker should be worn to keep the wind from your body. Not only will the gusts make you feel uncomfortable, they can hamper your skating starts. On colder days a hat may be a welcome addition. Heartier souls may don only a headband to keep their ears warm.

Indoors or outdoors, beginners should always wear gloves or mittens. Besides keeping the hands warm, they protect against ice burns in a fall.

Figure skaters usually are clad in a specific manner. Females wear flesh-colored tights with leotards or a short skirt. Most arenas and many dance and hosiery shops stock tights and skating outfits.

In skating competitions the dresses become fancier, with a wide variety of styles on display. Your outfit should reflect your personal taste.

Males cut the figures wearing stretchable slacks with a shirt or sweater. In competitions they may don stretchable jumpsuits.

Comfort is the first priority. Do not become overconcerned with fancy outfits, especially if you are just beginning. Keep in mind, it's how you skate, not how you look, that really counts.

General Safety Pointers

MANY TIMES a novice skater will find himself the cause of an ice accident. These collisions rarely stem from rudeness or a thoughtless attitude. More than likely, the person at fault simply has not learned the basic rules for safe skating.

The beginner must become familiar with these regulations. At most general skating sessions he will find himself joined on the crowded ice by intermediate-level and skilled skaters. *All* skaters have to practice basic safety rules in order to maintain a safe skating environment.

Before taking to the ice make sure skates are laced properly, to provide support. Lace ends should be tucked in and blade guards removed.

Whenever moving onto the ice, wait until the path is

clear. Do not charge out and cross in front of other skaters.

Skate calmly when on the ice. Don't barge past skaters ahead of you.

General sessions ordinarily require skaters to travel in a counter-clockwise direction around the rink. Always move in the same direction as the traffic flow. Wrongway skating is a main cause of rink collisions. Never swing around threading your way through oncoming traffic to locate friends or to leave the ice.

Always watch where you are going. Keep an eye out for other skaters. At anytime someone nearby may stumble, fall, or skate into your path. You may possess the reflexes and skating skill to avoid an accident, but you can react only if you see the trouble coming. Be alert at all times.

Don't follow on the heels of a very good skater. One of you could take a tumble. Even if a mishap is not in the offing, it simply isn't fair to interfere with other skaters.

Giving playful pushes to friends skating in front of you is a good way to cause collisions and falls. Remember, skate calmly. This is especially true when skating with a beginner. Don't annoy him or get in the way. At this point his balance is very delicate. Just think of the time you were in his skates and the difficulties you encountered before gaining confidence.

Most rinks have a barrier around the outer edge of the ice. It was not placed there for tired skaters to sit on or lean on while adjusting laces. Its main purpose is to provide beginners with a means of support. Novices would be wise to take advantage of this barrier by holding on with one hand while trying to skate. Don't grasp it with both hands and drag yourself around.

Figure skating requires the ability to skate in all directions. Advanced skating maneuvers should not be attempted until you've gained the skill to avoid less proficient skaters with little effort.

Many rinks reserve the center portion of the ice for those who wish to practice figures, jumps, and dance steps. Learn to skate competently around the outside of the rink before moving to the inner area. Beginners should not invade this territory. It will only serve to frustrate those working on difficult moves and increase the risk of injury to all skaters in the area.

Trying to practice edges or jumps during a crowded public session can present a problem. Beginners can easily get in the way. It is safer to work when good skaters are on the ice. They are able to control their moves, as well as anticipate where others will be going.

When competitive skaters are practicing at a general session have the courtesy to stay out of their path. Skaters working to music should be given the right of way. It may be prior to a competition and the skater might be working with music on a free skating routine. It is extremely difficult for a competitor to maintain the necessary concentration to execute a routine if he constantly has to keep an eye out for beginners. Giving up a few minutes of skating time will not cause you any real inconvenience. One day you may be the experienced ska-ter, and I'm sure you will appreciate others freeing the ice for you to practice.

Skaters wearing speed skates can be hazardous at pub-lic sessions. These skates are used mainly for racing, and the tendency is to travel at speeds that are unsafe on a crowded ice surface. The long blades present a constant threat to other skaters. Anyone near them can inadver-tently be kicked or tripped. The use of speed skates should be reserved for special speed skating sessions, or for a time when it is possible to work out alone.

Many rinks schedule special hours for figure skating, ice dancing, and speed skating. Arranging sessions in this manner makes it safer for everyone. If you arrive at the rink during one of these sessions, stay off the ice and wait for the general skate to begin.

If a guard is on duty on the ice, his authority should always be respected and his rules obeyed.

If an accident results in an injury, immediately notify the guard or someone at the rink box office. It is impor-tant to act quickly because you do not know the extent of the injury. The type of first aid required on the ice is the same as that administered in most recreational situations. Usually someone employed by the rink will be trained in first-aid techniques.

Although injuries do happen, beginners should not be frightened. The only thing a novice usually suffers in a fall is a slightly dented ego.

That First Time on the Ice

THE FIRST TIME a skater takes to the ice it is essential that the experience be a positive one. A mishap could create a negative attitude toward skating, which might result in a potential skater giving up before he really begins. Two catchwords for that first time on the ice are "slow" and "easy."

Before venturing onto the ice, check your skates. Have blade guards been removed? Many first-step falls are caused by forgetting this basic task. Are your skates properly laced? Make sure they provide sufficient support. You can get an idea of this simply by walking around on them, which is an exercise that will also accustom you to wearing skates. An experienced skater may make it look like the skate is part of the foot. It isn't. All skaters must get used to balancing on thin steel blades.

Are laces tucked in? Lace ends must never be allowed to drag on the ice. You, or another skater, could slip on them causing a nasty spill.

Put the fear of falling in its proper place. If you let the prospect of falling bother you, you will never fully develop skating skills. Everyone falls. No one is going to laugh at you. All skaters know how easy it is to take a spill. Falls are part of the sport, even in Olympic competition. Progress to more difficult movements and advancement as a skater include an occasional fall.

Now, to the ice:

Step onto the ice as if testing the water in a swimming pool, one foot followed by the other. Hold on to the barrier or the skates may run away. Pause for a moment without moving, simply to get a feel of the ice. Slide the skates forward and backward, keeping a firm grip on the barrier.

Don't be surprised when your ankles feel wobbly. You're not accustomed to balancing your entire body on two thin strips of steel. Make a conscious effort to hold the ankles firmly and as straight as possible.

Even though the glide in skating is very different from walking, beginners have the tendency to take a few steps on the ice. No harm will be done, and the skater will begin to get the feeling of what it is like to move on the ice.

A word of caution: there is a real possibility of slipping unless these steps are very short. Also, it is easy to trip over the toe picks, so make sure blades remain parallel to

34

the ice surface.

A "barrier pull" is a good way to get the feeling of gliding on the ice.

Turn the skates parallel to the barrier, knees bent and kept flexible in a position over the toes. Feet are 10 to 12 inches apart.

To gain motion, pull yourself hand-over-hand along the barrier. Maintain even weight distribution. This will provide a feeling of gliding.

If you happen to be in the company of two experienced skaters, they can take a light hold of each arm and gently pull you along to allow a supervised gliding experience.

When confidence and basic standing and gliding ability are achieved, it is time to let go of the barrier and begin skating unassisted.

Assume the basic skating posture:

Feet parallel to each other, about six inches apart.

Equal weight distribution.

Knees and ankles slightly bent with the pelvis riding directly over the feet.

Back is straight, with arms held comfortably out, waist high, at the sides; head and shoulders erect.

Start out with a few short steps, then glide on both skates.

You will immediately feel how the total body is involved in skating.

Try some more steps. This time lift each foot a few inches off the ice, so, for a moment, you are actually skating on one foot.

Basic skating posture. Feet are parallel, spaced six inches apart. Weight is evenly distributed. A slight bend in the knees and ankles positions the pelvis over the skates. Arms are held straight out, waist high. The head and shoulders are held erect.

Center weight over the skating foot and hold the skating ankle firm. You will quickly get the feet of shifting weight from one skate to another.

Practice this until you feel confident and totally acquainted with the ice.

It is now time to move into actual skating.

Falling and Getting Up

JUST AS forward and backward motion is integral to skating, an occasional downward flight should also be expected.

Rarely does a skating fall result in an injury. Especially when the skater knows how to fall. Knowing the proper way to take a tumble is an important facet of skating.

The key to a safe fall is to relax. When you feel yourself about to take a spill, relax and go with the fall. Bend the legs and allow the body to go limp. Let yourself "sink" into the ice.

The more you fight a fall, the more serious it will be. Relaxing reduces the chance of injury. If you take a tumble while in motion you will slide along the ice without any direct impact with the ice. A relaxed fall on the ice causes less discomfort than a misstep while on pavement.

Many beginners instinctively stiffen their bodies and swing the arms in an effort to regain balance. This usually assures a tumble.

Skaters can relieve their anxieties about falling by taking some practice spills.

Start out with forward falls. These can be safely broken by using the hands.

From a standing position on the ice, crouch down into a squat, with hands on the ice in front of you. Slide the hands forward as you straighten the knees. Keep your head up and allow the body to stretch out full on the ice. The impact of this fall will be taken on the chest and abdomen.

This practice fall is very similar to most forward falls. The major difference is that in unplanned tumbles you will be a greater distance from the ice.

When falling forward be sure to straighten the knees. Breaking a fall with the knees instead of the hands could be painful and cause serious injury to those joints. Many inexperienced skaters wear knee pads when learning new moves.

To get back on your feet, rise up on both knees, then place one foot's skate blade firmly into the ice and use your hands to thrust yourself up to a standing position.

To practice a backward fall, slowly move forward on both skates with arms in front of the body. Crouch down into a squatting position (try to make your knees touch

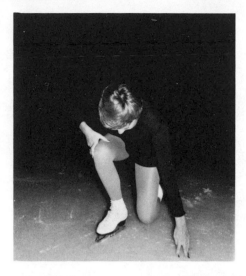

After a tumble, plant one skate firmly into the ice and raise yourself up to a standing position.

your chest). Sit back on the heels, getting your seat as close to the ice as possible. Slide both feet from under you, keeping arms and head forward. As you begin to fall, relax and go with the spill.

Get back on your skates quickly, in the manner previously described.

Breaking backward falls with the hands is unadvisable. Usually the hands do not slide out. They remain in place and absorb the full impact.

In backward falls the probability of hitting one's head on the ice increases. Never deliberately fall backward and allow your feet to slide out in front of the body.

To practice a backwards fall: begin a slight forward motion and assume a squatting position . . .

now let both skates slide out from under you and allow your body to go with the fall.

Most of the time there is no option in which way to fall, but keep in mind that forward falls generally are safer than backward tumbles. The potential for injury is reduced. Whenever possible, try to prevent throwing your weight backward.

Always be sure to get up as fast as possible after a fall. Then continue skating or leave the ice. Never remain sprawled or seated upright. Some skaters remain in a fallen position pretending to be hurt to hide their embarrassment, others take time out to laugh at their folly, still others just sit and pout. By remaining downed, you present a formidable obstacle for the skaters. Numerous accidents are caused by skaters coming into contact with fallen "icemen." Always get up quickly and keep moving.

One important point: make sure to get your fingers off the ice anytime you are down. Fingers on the ice are easily run over, especially at crowded public sessions.

Most competitive figure skaters are able to get up from a spill when jumping or spinning and continue without giving the miscue a second thought. They are able to fall and rise in one movement. Some skaters accomplish this as second nature, others will have to invest time practicing proper falling and getting up techniques before achieving this ability.

Falling in competition doesn't necessary mean all is lost. Much depends on how quickly you get up and carry on with the routine. Many times a skater is up so fast the fall is hardly noticed and doesn't break up the harmonious composition of the program.

Careless use of skate guards is a big cause of missteps. Always remember to remove these guards *before* taking to the ice. This will prevent a sure fall. Skate guards have no edges to provide necessary traction.

If you find yourself in this situation, remove the blade guards *while sitting* on the ice. Never try and get up and walk on the ice. Leaving the guards attached will only provide another opportunity to practice getting up.

It may be a silly error to make, and your ego may not be the only part of you to be bruised. But take heart, many skilled skaters have been guilty of the same error of omission. You are not the first, or the last, to try and glide on blade guards.

Sculling

As you begin to skate, it will be easier to travel around the rink with both skates remaining in contact with the ice. Two blades provide better balance. "Double sculling" is a method of skating on two feet.

Double sculling is accomplished by skating entirely on the inside edges of both blades.

Start forward double sculling with feet parallel and slightly apart, knees bent forward.

Turn skate toes outward and move the feet apart by applying an even amount of pressure to the inside edge of both skates.

Knees should straighten slightly, but not stiffen.

Turn the toes in and begin to bring the feet together in a parallel position.

Increase the knee bend as feet come back together.

Double Sculling. Knees and toes turn in to propel you across the ice.

Repeating the maneuver will produce forward motion. Make sure there is enough angle on each inside edge to grip the ice.

If the ankles are held too straight, edges will be too shallow and you won't be able to exert any pressure against the ice. This will result in slipping.

The farther your feet separate in the push, the faster and longer you will be able to travel.

Make the legs do the work. The arms are kept out from the body and held steady to maintain balance.

Double sculling is an excellent exercise to develop inside edges and leg power.

BACKWARD DOUBLE SCULLING

Learning to skate backward as soon as you can will be a great asset when moving on to figure skating. Most novices think skating backward means crashing into everything in their path. Actually, when properly done, backward skating permits as much visibility as skating forward. Do not become discouraged if your first backward strokes are ragged. Some find backward skating a simple task, while others encounter great difficulty.

Anytime backward skating is practiced without the aid of an instructor have someone keep an eye out for you until you gain good sightlines when traveling in this direction.

The easiest way to start skating backward is by backward sculling. Backward sculling should not be attempted until one feels comfortable while gliding backward on both skates. Gliding familiarizes one with the sensation of backward movement.

To glide, face the barrier with feet apart and knees bent to a point over the toes. The back is straight with head up. Do not look down at the feet. This will shift the point of balance and cause a forward fall.

Gently push away from the barrier and glide. Repeat. When you feel confident with the motion, begin work on backward double sculling.

Feet are placed apart with knees bent and the weight evenly distributed.

Head and shoulders are held squarely, with the arms out at the sides and hands at the hips.

Turn the heels out and toes in and move the feet slightly apart by applying even pressure to the inside edges. This will generate backward motion.

The knees should straighten a bit. The arms rise slightly to keep momentum and maintain balance.

Let the feet ride apart, but not so far as to be uncomfortable.

Turn the heels in and pull the feet back together to a parallel position.

As the feet come together, the knee bend increases and arms return to their original height.

Once you return to the original position, start again by turning the heels out and pushing the feet apart. This will make the in-and-out motion continuous.

A skater should get a definite feeling of pushing and pulling when double sculling. The push is felt as feet travel apart and pull as they come together.

Practice until you can double scull with an even, nonstop action.

SINGLE FORWARD SCULLING

Single sculling operates on the same basic principle as the two-foot maneuver. Now one skate performs the continuous motion while the other simply glides along on the flat of the blade.

Single sculling can be done on an alternate stroking basis, or on one foot for as long as you please.

This is a good stroking action for beginners to improve skating ability. Sculling will also be useful when skills have been sharpened.

Alternate sculling is an excellent warm-up exercise used by many advanced skaters when they take to the ice. It helps loosen up leg muscles and gets the kinks out of the knee joints.

Time invested in these maneuvers is well spent. They will improve control of power and balance in skating.

Stroking

STROKING IS THE traditional skating motion which propels the skater, forward or backward, across the ice. This is accomplished by a series of individual strokes. A thrust or "push-off" is made with one blade, followed by a glide on the other blade. Then the skate which was gliding pushes off and the other skate glides.

Proper stroking cannot be learned by imitating the motion of other skaters. Balance and body placement are essential components of stroking, and these components vary slightly from skater to skater.

The first step is a push forward and glide from a standstill.

Assume a "T" position, right foot forward with the instep of the left boot meeting the heel of the right boot.

Extend arms to the sides with shoulders and hips

The "T" position is implemented at the start of many figure skating maneuvers. To begin a basic forward glide . . .

push off the left inside edge by straightening the left knee.

square to the line of travel.

Shift weight back onto the left foot, turning that ankle slightly inward so only the inside skate edge is on the ice.

Bend knees deeply so the right bends forward as the left knee flexes.

For a basic forward thrust, push off the left inside edge by straightening the left knee while keeping the right knee bent. This straightening will force the edge into the ice to propel you forward.

Although it may seem easier to push off using toe picks, the thrust will be very weak. Also, the push and edge will be wobbly and allow for little power. Toe picks are to be used for certain stops, spins, and jumps, not thrusts.

As forward motion begins, body weight shifts to the right foot. This should be the entire body weight, not just the upper portion of the torso.

You are now in a forward glide.

Hold the left foot a few inches off the ice with the toes turned slightly outward. The right knee remains slightly bent with the kneecap pointing in the direction of travel.

The forward glide should be made in a straight line. Holding hips and shoulders square to the line of travel will insure the proper direction.

Hold the glide as long as you can, then bring the left foot forward to a point directly alongside the right. The right knee will have to straighten a bit to permit the left blade to remain clear of the ice as it passes the right foot. Not bending can cause a trip over the left toe picks.

Lower the left foot to the ice and glide on both blades.

That completes one forward thrust and glide.

Practice the same motion, this time have the left foot lead the "T" position with the right foot behind.

As you progress you will learn to use individual edges while stroking.

When the individual thrust and glide is mastered, a series of short strokes should be skated.

To work on a series, begin as before with the right foot gliding off a left-foot push. But now, when the left foot is brought alongside the right, let the right turn out to the side so the right inside edge pushes against the ice. Use the whole right blade to push onto a left glide.

When the feet come together in this movement they form a "modified T position" (in motion with a slight sideways angle).

Repeat the same procedures on the other foot.

This push and glide stroking motion makes it possible to continue skating around the rink.

Speed should be gained with each thrust.

A successful stroke is a smooth stroke. This is achieved by timing the bending of the knees with the shift of weight.

A series of strokes will quickly bring you to the end of the rink. There is no need to stop, simply end the last stroke on two parallel feet and turn the arms as if they are steering into the curve.

Glide with both feet together and lean with the whole body in a straight line into the turn.

This will also help give the feeling of skating on an edge.

Practice two-footed glides in each direction on the curve. From this glide you can skate directly into cross-overs.

Crossovers

CROSSOVERS ARE strokes used to travel on a curve. In some areas crossovers are called crosscuts.

FRONT CROSSOVERS

Stand in a "T" position with the left foot leading. Let the right arm and shoulder lean forward.

Push off into a left outside edge on a curve to the left.

Once the right foot leaves the ice it is carried past the left skate, crosses over the front of the left leg, and is lowered until it touches the ice.

At this point the feet are crossed and parallel. Weight shifts to the right foot.

The left skate comes off the ice with the toe pointed

To skate forward crossovers:
push off from a "T" position . . .

the right leg crosses in front of
the skating foot and lowers to the
ice . . .

feet are crossed and parallel
with the weight on (in this photo)
the right foot. Hold this position
for a short time . . .

then bring the left skate forward until it is next to the right boot . . .

now push off again and repeat the movements while negotiating the curve.

slightly inward.

Hold this position for a moment. Then let the left skate come forward and touch the ice next to the right skate.

Thrust forward with the right skate onto the left.

Repeat the movement as you continue traveling on a curve.

When skating in a circle, lean toward the center and do not vary your body angle.

Always bend the front knee and keep the degree of bend constant to gain a smooth stroke.

Always carry the left leg back behind the right skate following the crossing of the ankles.

This movement can be practiced by stepping out the procedure on the ground.

When you feel comfortable skating left crossovers, reverse the instructions to learn right crossovers.

Crossovers are an invaluable method of gaining speed in either direction. Mastering crossovers will prove a great asset when working on free skating programs.

BACK CROSSOVERS

This is very similar to the forward crossover. Before skating back crossovers, plan the moves thoroughly in your mind, or plot them out step by step on the ground.

First, skate backward to gain speed. Then glide backward in a curve to the left, with the left skate slightly forward in the direction of travel.

Weight remains on the right skate, which is on an outside edge.

The left arm is in front of the body, the right arm behind. The whole body is turned into the curve.

Thrust with the left foot and allow it to pass in front and across the right skate, ending in a position with the ankles crossed.

Weight now shifts over to the left leg.

The right foot comes slightly off the ice and is brought back across the front of the left skate. Keep it coming around until it is placed back on the ice a few feet inside the curve.

Lift the left skate slightly and swing it clockwise around the right skate, placing it on the ice parallel to the right foot.

This completes one crossover.

Repeat the circular movement and practice the crossover until the procedure is done smoothly.

By reversing the leg action, crossovers are done just as easily to the right.

At all times make sure the upper part of the body is turned toward the inside of the circle, and also be sure you can see in the direction of travel.

Greater knee bends and deeper, harder thrusts will result in greater momentum for the crossover.

These strokes are not just for use by beginners. Many skaters start a session with a series of fast forward strokes and crossovers in both directions. This is usually followed by some long, hard back crossovers in a giant figure eight pattern, also in both directions.

This gives the skater a feeling of skating and bending, and quickly warms him up.

If you attend a competition, try to get there early to watch the methods used by various skaters in the warm-up period.

Stops

IF YOU FIND YOURSELF crashing into the barrier or wrapping your arms around a fellow skater in order to stop, the thought may have occurred to you that "there must be a better way." Well, there is.

Stops involve a skidding action in which the edge of the blade cuts into the ice, shaving or scraping the surface. Friction slows and stops the skater. The rate of deceleration will vary according to original momentum and the stopping pressure applied.

Placement of the scraping skate, or skates, usually is done at a right angle to the direction of travel.

Develop your technique by stopping at slow speeds. Gradually increase momentum before the stop as ability and confidence are gained.

The simplest stops to learn are the snow plow, modified hockey stop, full hockey stop, and T-stop.

Give all four stops a try. Skaters differ as to which technique is most comfortable. What seems difficult to one skater may be easy for you.

SNOW PLOW

The braking action in this stop is accomplished by pushing the feet apart and turning the toes inward so that both blades skid on slight inside edges.

With feet together, face the barrier from an arm's length away. Grasp the barrier with both hands.

Bend knees, turn toes inward and push out on the heels so the skates move apart on slight inside edges.

Pull into the barrier with your arms. You shall find yourself skidding and shaving the ice surface.

Make sure even pressure is applied to both skates when pushing the blades apart.

If you have trouble making the blades slide, it could be caused by taking too much of an edge. Increasing the angle between the ice and the inner blade edge should clear up this problem.

When you feel comfortable with this stopping position at the barrier, begin using the snow plow on open ice at slow speeds.

Some skaters find a one-foot snow plow easier to master.

The initial position for this variation is the same as the

two-foot maneuver, but now only one skate toe is turned in and extended forward to shave the ice. Pressure is placed on this foot as the trailing foot remains in a straight skating line.

MODIFIED HOCKEY STOP

A quarter turn of the body and braking action (skid) by the leading foot on an inside edge are the elements of this stop.

Begin work on this method by facing and holding on to the barrier with both hands, feet together and knees bent. Place one foot (this will be the scraping or skidding foot) on a slight inside edge. The other foot assumes a deep inside edge for gripping the ice.

Slide the first foot away from the other, keeping pressure on the middle of the blade as it scrapes the surface of the ice. Skates remain parallel to each other. Body weight shifts in the direction of the sliding foot to create greater pressure on the blade into the ice. This causes increased friction and stopping power.

As the leading leg moves away, the rear leg straightens.

Practice this motion until you can apply steady pressure on the sliding foot. A good indication of this would be a small pile of snow developing from the shavings coming off the ice surface.

Now it's time to integrate the body turn. Turn your

body until your feet are parallel with the barrier. The sliding foot should be farthest from the barrier. With hands on the boards, turn your body toward the barrier as your sliding foot moves out. The inside foot acts as a pivot, turning and then rocking over onto an inside edge. Your final position will find body and feet facing the barrier.

Once you are able to make this move, it is time to begin stopping while in motion.

Glide slowly along the side boards, knees bent, skates parallel to each other on the flats of the blades. The sliding foot is away from the barrier.

Turn the body toward the boards as the sliding leg action is implemented. The final body position is facing the barrier.

A good knee bend is necessary to keep weight over the balls of the feet. Straight knees will shift weight onto the heels which could easily cause a fall.

Keep in mind that your stopping is a result of the scraping of the ice by the front foot. Be sure to apply effective pressure when pushing down into the ice.

If you have difficulty getting a good scrape from the front foot, it may be caused by the foot dropping into too much of an inside edge prior to the turn and skid. To remedy this situation, hold the ankles straighter before the turn, thus increasing the angle between the inside blade edge of the leading foot and the ice surface.

Once the modified stop is mastered, executing a full hockey stop will not be difficult.

Parallel blade position with shoulders facing the direction of travel are essential when doing a full hockey stop.

FULL HOCKEY STOP

Both skates now remain parallel and close together with the front foot on an inside edge and the rear foot on an outside edge.

Weight remains evenly distributed over both feet when making the turn.

Shoulders face squarely in the direction of travel, even when the hips and feet revolve in the quarter turn.

As the turn for the stop is made, a definite unweighting action takes place. This is accomplished by rising up a bit on both knees and shifting weight to the front of the skates as the body turns. Then sink back onto the knees with weight concentrated over the balls of the feet as you slide and stop.

Having skates turn and change direction instead of digging into the ice and stopping is a common problem. Holding the ankles straighter to create greater friction will get the blades to skid and stop.

T-STOP

This stop is done with the feet placed in a "T" position. The instep of the back foot forms a "T" with the heel of the front foot. Arms remain out to the sides, with shoulders facing squarely to the line of travel.

The scrape is made with the outside edge of the back foot as weight shifts from the front to the back skate. The front foot remains on the flat of the blade.

Many skaters encounter difficulty with this stop.

Common Problem No. 1. Skaters throw all their weight onto the back foot at one time. *Most* of the weight should shift to the rear foot. However, you cannot balance with all of your weight on just the rear skate.

Common Problem No. 2. The skater turns as he begins to stop. The front foot may be on an inside or outside edge. The lead blade must be kept on the flat. Also, the rear foot may not be positioned at a right angle to the front foot. This 90° angle is essential for a proper stop.

More advanced methods of stopping are one-foot stops, done on either edge of either skate. Once you can do the basic stops, modifying them into one-foot stops should be a simple matter.

Once the basic stops are mastered, many one-foot stops can be easily learned.

Turning

As soon as you are able to skate forward and backward it will be helpful to learn how to change direction.

There are many good techniques for reversing direction, and all employ the same four basics:

1. Straight posture to provide a firm, efficient axis of rotation. Any bend in the hips (upward, backward, or sideways) will throw off your balance and control.

2. A carefully timed bending and straightening of your knees.

3. A rotation of the upper body in the direction of the turn just prior to the actual move.

4. Counter rotation of the upper torso when coming out of the turn.

The easier turns to implement are those done on both skates. These can be practiced standing near the barrier.

Position the body so the left foot is closest to the barrier. Feet are close together on the flats of the blades.

With an erect posture, and knees slightly bent, turn the upper torso and head inward to face the boards. Place the right hand on the barrier in front of you and the left hand on the barrier behind you. The hands remain in this position throughout this exercise.

Relax the pressure on the skates and make a 180° forward turn by turning the feet and lower body toward the barrier.

The body should finish the turn in a "checked" position (arms and upper body facing against the direction just turned). Weight is centered over both blades.

Edges

FIGURE SKATERS must be able to master the four basic edges:

> Inside Forward Edge.
> Outside Forward Edge.
> Outside Backward Edge.
> Inside Backward Edge.

INSIDE FORWARD EDGE

This is probably the simplest of the edges to learn and should be the first of the four to be worked on.

Start in a "T" position with the right foot leading. The body is facing squarely ahead over the right foot. The right arm is forward and the left arm is out to your side. Both arms are held waist high.

Skate a few strokes. Try going around in a circle counter-clockwise while holding a right inside forward edge. You should be able to hold the edge under control for a full circle.

While on the circle the skating ankle and knee must be bent.

The free foot remains behind, carried directly over the tracing made by the skating foot.

Hips are placed forward under the body and always remain facing in the direction of travel. Thrust the skating hip ahead toward the center of the body so it feels hollowed in.

Shoulders are kept level and at a right angle to the line of the skating foot. Weight should be felt on the skating shoulder.

Turn the head over the free shoulder toward the center of the circle. Always remain conscious of the radius of the circle.

Once you are able to execute this move, reverse the body positions and try the same procedure on the other foot in the opposite direction. This would be skating on a left inside forward edge.

Check to see if you are pulling on the edge or making too small a curve. Two common errors will cause these problems:

1. Cutting too deep an edge. This is caused by leaning the upper body too far into the circle. Excessive leaning

takes too much of the body weight from the skate causing the skating hip to go off line. When this happens the skater will lose control of the curve.

2. Turning the free hip/leg/foot outward. This causes the skate which is cutting the edge to turn sharply into the circle. The centrifugal force created in skating this edge encourages the free leg to swing out across the print made by the blade.

This can be prevented by controlling the hips and shoulders. Do not let them swing around.

Constant awareness of the free foot's placement will also help eliminate these faults.

OUTSIDE FORWARD EDGE

This is one of the most important edges in the sport. Once you become adept at skating this edge, the body lean involved will make all areas of skating seem simpler.

Begin in a "T" position with the right foot leading.

The right arm is placed in front of the body with the left arm at the side at waist height.

Turn the head over the right shoulder.

Skate a few strokes and take a right outside forward edge around a clockwise circle.

Keep the back straight and hips tight. Lean the entire body to the right from the side of the blade.

Eyes should focus over the skating shoulder to be

aware of the angle of lean.

To control this move you must constantly press back on the free hip and leg, shoulder and arm. This assures that hips and shoulders will be in line with (or parallel to) the line of the circle.

The free foot should be turned out and pointed down. Carry it behind the skating foot and directly over the tracing. The free hip is turned out so that the inside of the free knee is angled toward the ice.

OUTSIDE BACKWARD EDGE

This edge begins with a right outside backward push.

Stand on both feet with skates slightly apart. The right foot is on an imaginary axis line (you might want to etch a line on the ice).

The left arm is in front with the right arm out to the side. Arms at waist height as usual.

Shift weight onto the left foot. As the weight is shifted, reverse the arm positions.

Give a good thrust with the left foot onto the right back outside edge and once again reverse the arms.

In order to skate a right outside back edge the body is turned halfway into the direction of travel, with the left foot extended behind. Muscles must be kept tense, especially in the free leg.

The free foot should turn out, pointing to the outside of the circle.

Weight constantly remains on the skating shoulder, which is carried higher than the free shoulder. If the unevenness in shoulder level is not maintained, you will skid and turn around with little control.

When you feel comfortable with the right outside backward edge, begin work on the left foot. Practice until you are able to skate both outside edges with speed and a good degree of lean.

Any skater who has hopes of becoming an accomplished jumper will find this maneuver most important, for a majority of jumps are landed on the outside back edge.

Skating a right outside back edge.

73

INSIDE BACKWARD EDGE

To get into this edge skate backward in a clockwise direction to gain speed. Then strongly cross over onto a right back inside edge. The free leg and foot move into a leading position on the curve.

When skating a right inside back edge, it's a good idea to "check" with your arms. ("Checking" is positioning arms in the reverse of the direction of movement. This helps in holding an edge and stops you from turning. Checking is also done on jump landings to stop the rotation.) In this case, have the left arm slightly in front pulling lightly backward on the right arm. If this is not done you may wind up with too much of a deep inside

74   *Skating an inside backward edge.*

back curve.

As in all these edges, this should be practiced on the other foot. Simply reverse body positions.

THE MOHAWK

The simplest forward-to-backward turn is the inside Mohawk.

The inside forward Mohawk is a turn made from an inside forward edge on one foot to an inside backward edge on the other foot. An outside Mohawk (outside forward edge to outside backward edge) can be done, but is quite difficult. At the outset, concentrate on the inside maneuver.

Begin by standing in the "T" position, right foot lead-

To skate an inside Mohawk, push off into a firm inside forward edge . . .

draw the heel of the free foot, with the toe turned out, to the skating foot . . .

and step over to a left inside back edge as the right skate comes off the ice.

ing with the right arm and shoulder in a forward position.

Push off into a firm right inside forward edge. Keep the skating knee well bent with body weight just back of the center of the blade.

Press the free arm and shoulder and the free skate onto the line of the print.

Bend the free knee and draw the free foot, heel first, toward the skating foot. Turn the toe outward as much as possible. Now, simply step over to the left inside back edge with the right foot coming off the ice behind.

As the turn is executed, reverse the pressure on the shoulder blades as the body turns to the left. This happens as weight shifts from one foot to the other. The transition of weight must be smooth and quick to do a successful Mohawk.

The lift to a straight knee as you turn is very important in achieving a smooth, clean turn.

The most difficult element of the Mohawk is to synchronize the timing of the free-foot and leg turn with the weight shift. If the turn is too slow, or the weight shift too early, the Mohawk will be scraped.

It should appear that you are naturally stepping from one foot to the other as the body does a half-turn.

Mohawks are skated equally well off either foot.

OUTSIDE FORWARD THREE TURN

One foot turns are more difficult to execute than those skated to two feet. The outside forward three turn is the

The number "3" etched into the ice is the result of a well-skated Three Turn.

easiest of the one-foot turns.

The three turn earned its name for a very logical reason; the pattern traced on the ice resembles the number 3.

This turn is the best known in figure skating because it is used at the beginning of ice waltzes and many free skating maneuvers. It also plays an important part in school figures (compulsory figures).

To start a right outside forward three turn, get in a "T" position with a right-foot lead.

Push off onto a strong right outside forward edge. Allow the left arm and shoulder to swing forward while keeping the right arm back.

The skating hip is held in tight underneath the body. Body weight should be felt pressing down onto the skating ankle and foot. Press the free leg and hip back so they are in line with the circle.

Rotate shoulders in a motion against the hips until the shoulder line is approximately square to the skating foot.

This rotation, in combination with a strong lead, will make the turn possible with minimal effort.

Lower the free leg and foot to a ''T'' position behind the skate.

When the feet touch, shift weight to the ball of the skating foot and increase backward pressure on the skating shoulder.

These movements allow the body to pivot with the skating side serving as the axis.

Always have control of the skating knee as it pushes off with a strong forward bend and gradually straightens as the turn approaches. The knee bends once again after the turn.

After the turn you will be skating on an inside back edge.

Check your arm slightly against the rotation. Failure to do this will prolong the turn. Don't forget to shift weight on your skate.

Half the leading skate must lift off the ice in any one-foot turn. Skating on the whole blade will always cause scraping of the ice, or sticking, which will prevent a smooth completion.

Spread Eagle

SOME SKATERS find the spread eagle easy to master, others have great difficulty gaining the proper technique. All skaters will agree that when done correctly this is one of the most beautiful maneuvers performed on ice.

To assume an absolutely correct position on this edge one must have very limber hip joints. While off ice, work on basic turnouts, such as the ballet first or second position, to gain body flexibility.

Begin work on the spread eagle while holding on to the barrier or railings.

Slide both feet to each side. Press the toes out and around to the sides as far as you possibly can, pressing the heels forward at the same time.

Keep both knees bent and drop both ankles strongly over onto the outside edges until the outsides of the boots touch the ice.

Now slowly straighten the knees and pull the derriere up under your body.

Keep the ankles dropped. Do not arch or pull in the back muscles. This will cause a swayback position, which shows poor form and is potentially harmful. Keep the rear end tucked under the body.

Stay as straight as possible. Concentrate on the straightness of the knees and turnout of the toes.

Push yourself along the rail, or have a friend push and lend support. Practice in this manner until you feel comfortable balancing in this position.

These basics still apply when the spread eagle is done in motion.

There are two ways of getting into the edge for the spread eagle.

1. Accelerate, then glide on both skates. With a gliding motion try to force either the left or right (whichever feels easier) skate in front of you while the other foot quickly flips, toes out, into a straight line behind the lead skate.

As the feet slide out the body will naturally turn sideways.

Press the leading shoulder back and allow the following arm and shoulder to come around the curve.

Unless you are a natural you will have to hold your ankles partially dropped over the outside to maintain the proper position until you become limber enough to curve to the outside.

At first you will probably succeed in making a straight line, or even a reverse curve, if the skate is not fully turned out. Just keep practicing.

2. This method is more effective but will require a bit more initial courage.

Skate an outside forward edge on whichever skate you have chosen to lead.

Swing the free leg and foot, first forward, and then back, with a vigorous turnout so that the skate takes to the ice behind you, slightly outside the line of the leading skate. Placing the trailing skate in this position will be very effective, especially if the heel is placed far forward with the toes turned as far back as possible. This forces the skates to start a proper curve to the outside.

Keep the ankles dropped to the outside until you have enough speed to lean the whole body into the curve.

Be careful not to place the feet too far apart. This will create too much strain on the knees. Approximately two feet is the correct distance between heels. This may vary, depending on the length of a skater's legs.

While in the move, pull up on all the muscles, especially those in the abdomen and diaphram.

Remember, the spread eagle can only be done correctly with a lot of speed and straight body lean from the edge of the blades.

When you are adept at this on an outside edge, you may want to switch over to an inside edge. A large inside circle spread eagle is very difficult to control. A small circle spread eagle will not aid in gaining limberness.

Some people have naturally turned-in hips. They will never be able to achieve a perfect spread eagle. Which does not mean they should avoid this move. Whether done beautifully or not, it is an excellent maneuver to use in practicing the turnout.

Since points are awarded for grace and beauty, oftentimes the shape of the skater's legs will add to the loveliness of the finished product.

Concentrate on the spread eagle until you have it mastered. Daily practice is the only way to gain the ability to skate the move with great ease. There is nothing more beautiful than the spread eagle when done with a graceful backward lean.

Rolls

ROLLS ARE semicircles skated first on one foot, then the other, along the same axis. Rolls are done on outside forward, inside forward, outside backward and inside backward edges. These four rolls are the basis of the school figures and free skating exercises. They are required in the preliminary figure skating test and will prove a great asset when beginning work on the basic figures.

Before starting rolls, etch a straight line in the ice using the heel of the skate blade. Many rinks have red and blue lines (for hockey) on the ice and these can also be used.

OUTSIDE FORWARD ROLL

Begin in the "T" position with the toes of the right skate touching the line at a right angle, the left skate is behind and perpendicular to the right boot.

Arms, shoulders, and hips are positioned as if a regular outside forward edge is to be skated (right arm in front and left arm at the side).

Push off into a firm, leading right outside forward edge. After gliding a short distance, slowly swing the left foot and leg in front of the right foot. At the same time reverse the arms, passing them close to the body.

The complete change to this second position should take a few counts. A definite lean to the right must be maintained.

As the left leg is brought from the back to the front, the skating knee gradually straightens.

By this time you should have completed a half-circle and will be approaching the line.

Drop the left foot back beside and parallel to the skating foot. The blade should actually touch the ice.

As this movement is executed, both knees bend and the right foot turns out a full quarter turn to the right and pushes to the original position. This is done on a left outside forward edge at a right angle to the line.

Now repeat these movements with the left skate as the skating leg and the right as the free skate. Make sure to include the rhythmic bending and straightening of the skating knee while on the left edge.

Continue alternating left to right all the way down the ice. It's a good idea to count to yourself in a slow waltz tempo to keep an even cadence of motion.

The push from the line should always be done with the entire blade. Toe picks are not to be used for this purpose. Clean starts from a whole blade are necessary for success in preliminary or any figure skating tests.

It is important for control that the free hip does not rotate forward as you pass the free foot and leg forward in a *close* passing movement. Keeping the free leg near as it is brought to the front minimizes the pull and allows a constant lean to be maintained. If the pull is too great, the size of the circle will be too small.

The length of edges on rolls (diameters of circles) should be approximately three times the height of the skater. This is the generally accepted size of the circle that should be skated when doing a figure eight. At this point in a skater's development, however, circle size is not as important as gaining real control of the skating edge.

INSIDE FORWARD ROLL

Inside rolls are skated with the same basic technique as outside edge rolls.

Begin in the "T" position with the right foot in front,

perpendicular to the line. The left foot is behind and parallel to the line. The left arm leads with the right to the side at waist height.

Push off into a right inside forward edge.

At the halfway point of the roll, reverse the leg and arm position.

In this maneuver, keep the same bend-and-rise knee motion and upright posture as in the outside edge roll.

Hips face squarely forward. You should feel the weight on your inside skating shoulder, with the free hip under you.

The front of the free foot should feel as if it is pressing to the outside of the circle.

As the free skate passes, lean back a small amount. A slight backward lean balances the weight of the free leg in front and should be done on inside and outside rolls to maintain an even balance over the back of the blade.

Continue alternating left to right all the way down the ice.

OUTSIDE BACKWARD ROLL

This roll is a bit trickier than the others. The starting position is altered, and you will have to learn a back outside push.

Start by facing down the axis line with the right foot on the line and the left foot slightly behind. Feet are parallel to each other. The left arm is in front with the right arm

The back outside push. The right skate lifts just off the ice . . .

the arm position is reversed as the left leg thrusts, making a complete arc, . . .

the arms again reverse, and, as the right foot comes into contact with the ice, the left skate takes a position over the print in front of the right skate . . .

on the second push in the roll you will be on a right back edge with the right arm in front.

just behind the body. Weight distribution is even.

Bend the right knee to push off, then shift weight over to the left leg with a fairly deep bend on the left knee. Lift the right foot to a point just off the ice surface, slightly out to the side, and reverse the position of the arms.

Thrust with the left leg, allowing it to make a full arc on the ice. Step onto the right foot and once again reverse the arm positions.

There is a double arm movement and double knee bend.

As the right foot hits the ice, the left skate, which has completed the push, lifts and moves directly on top of the print in front of the right skate. This is the same move as in a regular back stroke. This deep back sitting position (hips square, free arm forward, skating arm back, head facing inside the circle) is held for three counts.

Change into an outside back edge body position (free leg behind as on the basic roll) on counts 4–5–6. Make sure body lean to the right is maintained as the position changes.

Head position is changed from looking inside the circle to looking outside, and you are skating on a regular outside back edge. Make sure the arm placement is square, with the right arm across the body as you approach the axis line for the next push.

On the next push the entire procedure is repeated. The difference is that now you have already established momentum (no standing start) and the arm position is switched in a 1–2 cadence with the push. You will be on a right back edge with the right arm in front. As the foot turns to make the push the arms switch position. The left arm should be in front as the foot hits the ice. As the right foot pushes off, once again the arms reverse.

The arms are now in the same position as they were prior to the push (right arm in front, left behind).

The same procedure is repeated skating on the left foot.

INSIDE BACKWARD ROLL

Begin by having your back face along the line, in the direction you will be traveling. The right foot is on the line, the left foot is parallel to the right, spread about 1½ feet. The right arm is in front, the left slightly behind. The same type of push as in the back outside roll is employed, except that now the right toe turns inward to make the beginning of the half-circle with the left foot pushing off behind.

As soon as the push is made, the left arm comes to the front, right to the back, and you will be looking over your left shoulder into the center of the circle.

The hips should be held firm, and the free leg in front. Do not let yourself roll off this edge too soon, or the circle will be too small.

As you travel around the circle, slowly move the free leg close behind the other leg, and bring the arms tightly around to the body. The right arm must be held tightly across the front of the body. The left arm is extended behind. Be sure not to swing the arms, or control will be lost.

As you prepare for the push onto your left foot, the original movements are repeated; the right foot turns and the left foot hits the ice at a perpendicular angle to the long axis by turning in the toe. Keep the same rhythm as in the first push.

Backward edges are not easily mastered, but you will see the dividends of your effort when you begin to work on figure eights.

Jumps

JUMPING, whether from a diving board, ski run, or off the ice, is the closest a human can come to unassisted flight. That breathless second of poised suspension in the air is the jumper's objective.

Many youngsters think that jumping is the only part of figure skating. By this time you should realize this is hardly the case!

Learning to jump is part of the natural progression of figure skating ability. However, even with on-ice coordination, jumps should not be attempted until control of edges has been mastered. Once the control of skating on edges has been acquired, jumping will not be difficult to learn.

Many beginners have a fear of leaving the ice. Don't worry. Nervousness disappears as soon as work on the simplest jumps has begun. Don't attempt complicated leaps until you are able to do the easy ones with good takeoffs and landings.

One way to achieve that feeling of flying is to begin jumping while off ice. If you can do a jump on the ground, without the speed and flow that the skates will provide, imagine the elevation you can achieve using the ice as your springboard!

For a successful takeoff you will need a fast edge and plenty of elevation. The knees must bend deeply for quick spring, while the body and head remain erect and centered. Keep the back straight. Drawing the diaphram out by breathing in at the moment of takeoff will help in supplying lift.

Skating jumps fall into two categories:

1. "Edge Jumps." Jumps with a takeoff from one foot's running edge.

2. "Toe Jumps," or "Tap Jumps." Jumps with a takeoff from the toe point of the free foot. The toe point serves as the lever at takeoff.

Split-second timing of the placing of the toe pick and the moment of lift are essential ingredients for a successful toe jump. Jumping before the tap, or too late, will ruin the move. Try segmenting the preparatory moves: the edge before the Mohawk (or three turn), the turn in, the edge out, the actual spring.

The action of the toe point leg is vitally important to the elevation, but the main lift comes from the straightening of a well-bent skating knee.

94

The skate must remain on a good running edge. There should be no scraping of the toe point before the jump. Not only does scraping make an unpleasant noise, it impairs the smoothness and freedom of the jump, as well as essential speed.

One skill that is needed to execute different jumps is the ability to turn the body while in the air.

How do you make yourself revolve in midair? By the use of arms and shoulders and the jumping leg after takeoff.

For a half, or whole turn, nothing more than a simple reversal of the arms and shoulders is necessary. Flailing the arms or pulling them in an exaggerated fashion is not needed and will do more harm than good.

It is important to remember that arms and shoulders should not turn until the body has left the ice. In all jumping takeoff positions the shoulders must be held *against* the revolution until the split second of the spring.

The body must remain one coordinated unit throughout the jump. The upper body cannot break the curve, nor can the legs. There must be no forward break of the body at the hips or waist while skating on the takeoff edge.

Before takeoff, body weight must remain back, and then shift forward up over the takeoff foot at the moment of thrust.

Proper use of the toe pick is essential for graceful jump landings. Landing directly on the flat of the blade is improper form. You must return to the ice with a roll off the toe pick into a cushioned landing on the ball of the foot. In order to accomplish this, a specific sequence must take place: initial contact is made with the toe pick, then the ball of the foot, winding up on an edge of the entire blade.

Too much toe pick will dig into the ice, making an unsightly gash as well as an unpleasant scratching sound. In addition, a toe pick placed too deeply in the ice will cause a considerable loss of momentum. Well-landed jumps retain as much speed as the takeoff.

The proper jump landing position.

EDGE JUMP CHART

Here is a rundown of the edge jumps, indicating the takeoff and landing edges, and the number of revolutions turned in the air. These moves are based on a counterclockwise rotation.

Jump	Takeoff Edge	Landing Edge	Rotations
Waltz Jump	LFO	RBO	½
Axel	LFO	RBO	1½
Double Axel	LFO	RBO	2½
Salchow*	LBI	RBO	1
Double Salchow	LBI	RBO	2
Triple Salchow	LBI	RBO	3
Loop	RBO	LBO	1
Double Loop	RBO	LBO	2
Triple Loop	RBO	LBO	3
Walley	RBI	LBO	1
Half-Loop	RBO	LBI	1
Inside Axel	RFI	RBO	1½
One-Foot Axel	LFO	LBI	1½

L = Left
R = Right
B = Back
F = Forward
O = Outside
I = Inside
* All Salchows can be entered from a left forward outside three turn or a Mohawk right to left.

All jumps should be done on a slight curve, but not so tight that you appear to be jumping around yourself. Learn to land the jump with your edge on a wide angle curve that matches the takeoff curve. It should be a natural flow. This can be practiced on the floor by bending and jumping off both feet and using the arms to rotate the body. Many ballet dancers can successfully complete two or three in-air rotations.

Jumps should give the appearance of being flexible and soft. Flexibility in a jump is achieved by having perfect balance at the instant of landing. Using the knee as a shock absorber will make all landings look more graceful. One reason for a broken landing on a jump would be turning out the skating hip. Leaning out of the circle can also cause an awkward landing.

Landings are most important. In competition, jumps are judged first by *control of the landing edge*. Correct takeoff, elevation, and position in the air are additional judging factors.

THE BUNNY HOP

The simplest jump to learn is the bunny hop. When well done, with speed and good elevation, this jump is quite impressive. Skaters of all ages should be able to master this jump.

The jump is simply a forward leap from the flat of one skate to the toe pick of the other, then back to the flat of

The ankle flexes, and up you go in the Bunny Hop. The free leg comes forward as the skating leg (left leg) kicks back to form a semi-split at the top of the jump.

the original takeoff skate.

Start out with a few short strokes for speed. Take a straight left forward edge with the skating knee well bent and the free leg extended behind.

Spring quickly, flexing the ankle. This will permit you to lift straight up from the picks of the left skate. At the same time the free leg (right leg) swings straight forward and past the left leg.

As the left leg leaves the ice, kick it slightly backward. The legs will then be in a semisplit position at the top of the leap.

99

Body weight now shifts onto the right toe point.

As you now begin the descent to the ice at a point not far from the takeoff, bend the right knee for impact. As the left leg comes forward past the right toe point, push off onto the flat of the left blade and glide away. The toe point and edge landing should be simultaneous.

During the bunny hop, the arms should swing naturally with the jump, but never rise above the shoulder line. The shoulders should not rise at all. Not on the bunny hop nor on any other jump.

Now practice this hop from the right flat to the left toe point, and back to the right flat.

WALTZ JUMP

This is the first fundamental edge jump (also called a three jump). You should master this jump before beginning work on the more difficult axel, axel Paulsen (named after its inventor), and double axel jumps.

The waltz jump is done on a wide skating arc.

The takeoff for the waltz jump is from a left outside forward edge. A half-turn is done while off the ice, landing on the outside back edge of the right foot.

At the top of the jump allow the body weight to shift forward toward the right side. This will permit the half-revolution.

You should land softly over the ball of the right foot. All jump landings are made on the ball of the foot, never

The take off for a Waltz Jump. The forceful swing of the arm and leg generates greater power for a more spectacular jump. This is also the take-off position for the Axel Jump.

on a scratched toe pick, or too far back on the heel.

Work up to doing a full waltz jump. Practice the basics of the jump by stepping from a right outside forward edge to a left outside back. As you gain confidence, take a slight knee bend and jump the edge. You will soon be jumping longer distances and higher elevations.

AXEL JUMP

The axel is basically the same as the waltz jump, only an

extra revolution is added. This is accomplished by a greater takeoff knee bend and more thrust with the free leg. The arms are pulled in for greater rotation. Because of this extra revolution, be sure to check the landing and control the edge.

SALCHOW

This is one of the easiest of the edge jumps. Although not difficult to learn, many skaters find gaining any degree of consistent perfection elusive when skating this maneuver.

The take off for the Salchow. The free leg swings wide to provide lift on the jump.

The jump is named for its inventor, Ulrich Salchow.

It usually starts from a left outside forward edge, turning a three turn onto a left inside back edge with the free leg allowed to swing back.

Now the free leg does the work. Let it swing in a wide arc around to the front. While carried by the momentum of the free leg, spring off the left knee. The right arm and shoulder should also follow this motion.

After completing a three-quarter turn in the air, land in a basic finishing position on a right outside back edge.

The whole jump should be carried out easily and effortlessly. Avoid a heavy scratch with the toe picks on the single Salchows. Miscues on the more advanced double and triple Salchows will turn that scratch into an enormous rip in the ice.

BALLET JUMP

When done properly, the elementary leap gives the appearance of an advanced maneuver. It makes a lovely picture, takes little daring, and depends on good form for its effect. The ballet jump can be learned by skaters of any age.

Begin from a right outside back edge. Point the left toe into the ice, at the same time bending the left knee. Allow some body weight to shift onto the left leg.

Spring from both legs.

As your body shoots straight up into the air, lift the right leg. It should be turned out and pointed high in back. Stretch the left leg straight down and slightly forward.

Land on the left toe point, pushing off to a standard right inside forward edge.

Try the same jump in the opposite direction. Begin with a left outside back edge. It is not a difficult jump to do in reverse position.

Your arms may strike a variety of poses in the air. Both may be over your head, or in various ballet positions, etc.

Before trying the ballet jump on the ice, study all the positions in front of an off-ice mirror. It will give you a good idea of the effect of the jump.

MAZURKA JUMP

This is a variation of the ballet jump. In the mazurka, the

As the legs cross in the Mazurka, the arms can assume a variety of graceful positions.

legs cross while in the air. After the tap, the right toe comes across the left and both feet are drawn together.

Implement the same takeoff as in the ballet jump, only now the right leg comes across after a left pick. Then the legs release for the same 1–2, right-toe, left-edge landing.

SPLIT JUMP

This toe jump highlights body flexibility. When the jump is done with good elevation and a hip-high split, it is most exciting to see. The split jump can be done at any level of skating.

The takeoff position is the same as the Mohawk (right inside forward to left inside back). The right toe picks in and the feet ride together at takeoff. The left leg kicks forward as the right snaps straight back from the hip. Each leg turns out and points.

The left arm can pass across the body as it turns forward in the direction of flight of the takeoff. The right arm flings back and remains in that position, even as you land.

The left toe point is first to touch the ice, followed by a right inside forward edge. Let the left skate land naturally without reaching for the ice.

The keys to a successful split jump are keeping the back straight on takeoff and maintaining perfectly even balance between the two legs while in the air.

Leaning forward with hips back, or any break in posture, will ruin the timing and balance of this or any toe jump.

Overreaching on takeoff with the toe point leg, causing a separation of the hips, is fatal to a quick, strong elevation.

Make believe a large rubber band is holding your hips together. When you take off the only stretching to be done is with the free ankle and knee.

Your split jump will only be as good as your ability to do a split. Practice splits on the floor to increase limberness.

An exciting variation of the split jump is the Russian split, which is a sitting split, with hands touching feet.

Jumps have various landing positions and are done in numerous combinations. Ability as a skater determines the complexity of maneuvers. A beginner may be able to do only the simplest jumps, but these can still be combined into a pleasing routine.

Here is a simple combination. Begin with a waltz jump, landing on a right outside back edge.

From that edge, take off into a half-loop jump, landing on a left inside back edge.

Allow the free leg to swing around into a single Salchow jump.

This is a combination of elementary jumps that can be effectively learned by a novice jumper.

No matter how much time you spend on the ice, continue to practice jumps on the ground. Working from a still position on the floor will improve rotation ability, as well as control of landings.

Another method to use to master a jump is to practice one leap in succession. If you are working on an axel jump, try to do two axels in a row. This improves stamina and increases mobility. You will now find yourself able to do different jumps (or the same one) one after the other.

Beginning jumpers should learn to do simple jumps in both directions.

Many jumpers learn all jumps in a single direction. They seem to have great difficulty changing direction. Learning two ways from the start will eliminate this problem and enable you to master complicated jumps in two directions.

Competitions are getting stiffer and stiffer, so being able to do things both ways gives you greater options to plan exciting and varied routines.

Spins

TWIRLING ON THE ICE is a move which is fun for skaters to execute and exciting for spectators to watch.

There is one factor that can take all the enjoyment out of skating spins: dizziness. It's no fun feeling as if you are still whipping around the arena after your body has stopped.

In most cases dizziness can be avoided. Try this:

As you begin to spin, look straight out at eye level. Do not look up or down. Allow the eyes to focus normally.

Learn to center a spin with the body straight, rotating on one spot on the ice. Shoulders remain level with the head and body, which are kept perfectly still as you spin.

Keeping the body straight is a most important point. Beginners have a tendency to rock themselves forward, back, sideways (or all three) as they initiate a spin. This is an excellent way to feel what it's like to be in a row boat during a sea storm. Keep your body straight and it should be smooth sailing during those spins.

To end the spin, let the arms and free leg release, and jab the toe point of the free foot into the ice. At the same time give your head a good toss to clear away the dizzies.

Every skater has a natural preference for one direction to spin and jump. For example, many righthanded skaters like rotating to the left. Before you begin to spin and jump, find out your most comfortable turning direction.

DOUBLE FLATFOOTED SPIN

This two-footed spin is the simplest spinning maneuver. When done properly, large ringlets will be traced on the ice.

The double flatfooted spin is entered from back crossovers, with a deep right inside back edge. The free arm swings way forward and the free foot flows back across the print the skating foot was etching. This wind-up will give you rotation in the spin.

The point of balance is kept at the center of both blades. Spin on both feet using the rotation gotten from the right back inside edge. Pulling the arms in should allow free rotation. If the feet are in the proper position it will feel as if they are chasing each other.

Body weight remains distributed over both skates.

Winding up for a double flat-footed spin . . .

a strong armswing provides increased speed of rotation . . .

with the center of balance directly on both skates.

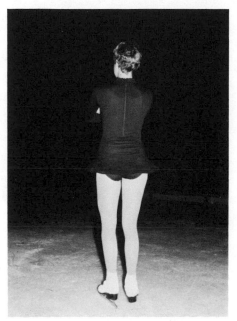

There should be no movement of the feet, or body trunk, once the spin has begun.

Start with the arms out shoulder high to each side (you may want to clench your fists to prevent a rush of blood to the fingers).

After several turns, curve the elbows and draw your fists in front of you in a circular motion. This should be a gradual "fighting" move. One set of muscles pulls, and another resists the pull. You are "fighting" yourself. This creates extra force to pull into a fast spin. You are

111

also fighting against centrifugal force.

Once the hands meet they draw into the chest with elbows bent out. From this position the hands slowly push straight down, close to the body.

As the arms push down, shoulders push down as well. The head pushes back up against this movement. Abdominal muscles are pulled in, the diaphragm out. This is the only body movement that will not upset your balance.

When you do it properly you can maintain a long, fast spin. This method of holding speed is common to all fast standing spins.

When you begin to work on this move, you may find it difficult to enter the spin from that inside back edge. Instead, give yourself a single push into a right inside forward edge. Snap up on both feet, allowing the left foot to toe you into place.

SINGLE FLATFOOTED SPIN

The ability to spin on the flat of one blade is basic to all other spins, and must be done with speed before moving on to any fast toe spins.

Entry into the single-foot spin is similar to the double spin. But when you reach the point where you want to turn, straighten up sharply. Center your balance on the balls of the feet, on the absolute flat of the blades. Do not let the skates turn at all.

Center up while the body is still traveling forward.

You should not be on either edge as you spin.

Entering a one foot spin . . .

pulling in the arms and free leg increases the speed of rotation.

As you center from the strong outside forward edge, swing the outer free leg forward, wide, and high. Keep it straight out from the hip to the right side as you begin to spin.

As the arms are drawn in for speed, bend the free knee with the foot straight down at a right angle with the knee. The free knee is bent until the free foot is placed directly behind the spinning knee. This is a resistance move. Pulling in the free leg creates the same sort of resistance as previously done with the arms and will provide tremendous speed.

With steady balance, speed and length of spin can be increased by dropping the free foot slowly down the spinning leg until both feet are closed together. Pressure must be kept on the spinning leg's shoulder, but the upper body does not turn.

One absolute necessity for a good spin, possibly the most important factor, is the ability to keep a straight spinning knee. One of the most common faults of beginning skaters is spinning with a bent skating knee. Beware, this is a most difficult habit to break.

All spins should revolve in one spot. Learning to spin with a bent spinning knee means you will not be able to revolve in a stationary place. It also makes it exceedingly difficult to keep from rocking back and forth.

Straighten the spinning knee as much as possible. Even if it means springing into a locked position.

Have a friend watch you spin. It is very hard to determine on your own if the knee is remaining straight.

To become a versatile spinner you must learn to spin in

the same rotation on the other foot. This is called a back spin. The back spin is done either on an outside back, or inside forward edge, rather than on an inside back and/or outside forward edge.

There are many variations of the basic flat spin. These include the sit spin, done in a sitting position; and the beautiful camel spin, done in an arabesque position.

Spins are done in numerous ways; from different positions, edges, jumped takeoffs changing edges, etc. A skater may begin a spin in one position, then go directly into a second position.

To explain all the spins and variations would require an extensive volume on this one aspect of skating. As you progress, you will pick up many new spins.

All figure skaters, and especially anyone thinking of skating in competition, should strive to become competent spinners. A well-executed spin gives spectators and judges quite a thrill.

Into a sit spin. A beautiful variation of the single flatfooted spin.

Spiral

THE SPIRAL IS one of the most graceful and beautiful free skating moves. A simple definition of a spiral is "a glide in an arabesque position." The skater glides on one leg while the other is extended high and behind. The position is derived from classical ballet.

The beauty of a spiral lies in several of its facets; the

The spiral is a glide in an arabesque position. The free leg is extended with the foot turned outward. The body is horizontal to the ice.

116

speed with which it is done, the arch and position of the free leg and arms, and the flow of the curve.

Spirals can be skated forward or backward, on either edge, and with an infinite variety of arm positions.

To begin work on the spiral, start with the forward position, either as an off-ice exercise, or on the rink while holding on to the rail.

The free leg must be stretched, with the foot turned out. The extension of the leg will increase with practice. The body trunk should remain as horizontal to the ice as possible.

Once this move can be confidently executed at the rail, try it in motion, gliding straight down the ice or around a

The Charlotte Spiral is a variation of the basic spiral. In this move you need a lower body position with higher leg extension.

117

curve. Don't forget to work on this position on the other foot, as the spiral can be done on either leg.

It is most important that the spiral be firm and steady. You can do all the head and arm movements you desire, but the free leg must remain absolutely motionless.

Getting into Figure Skating

IN MOST PARTS of the United States figure skating is a well-organized sport. Its governing body is the United States Figure Skating Association (U.S.F.S.A.). Rule books with information on competition regulations, test requirements, as well as other pertinent facts about amateur skating can be obtained by contacting the U.S.F.S.A., Sears Crescent, City Hall Plaza, Boston, Massachusetts 02108. Your local skating club is another good source for information about the sport.

Most countries have their own skating associations. The sport is controlled on an international level by the International Skating Union (I.S.U.).

Any skater wishing to enter competitions must first become a member of a figure skating club to be eligible to take the various tests as well as enter skating contests.

Joining a club is also a great way to meet new friends who share your interests, as well as enabling you to participate in club sessions specifically set aside for figure skating.

SKATING TESTS

There are nine figure skating tests, beginning with the preliminary, then progressing through tests one to eight (eight being the gold medal). Earning that gold medal requires years of practice and concentration.

Each test consists of different compulsory figures. The preliminary includes the basic edges and rolls. The gold medal includes intricate figures used in international and Olympic competition.

In addition to the compulsories, a free skating program of a specified difficulty, and incorporating certain moves, is required on the fourth, sixth, and eighth tests.

Competition divisions are categorized as to skating ability expected in each test classification (preliminary level skaters compete against each other, sixth level skaters against each other, etc.). Gold medal status is an eligibility requirement for world or Olympic competitions.

Each country has its own test standards, and there are also a set of four tests regulated by the International Skating Union.

Beginning skaters won't be qualified for these formal

exams, but can start by taking tests offered by local rinks. The Ice Skating Institute of America has an excellent series of graduated basic tests.

Whatever testing program you become involved in, remember it is more important to improve your skating ability than to receive a passing grade.

Don't be overdisappointed if you do not pass a specific exam. Some of the top skaters have had to take their tests more than once. Failing a test simply points out certain areas that need additional practice. After some more work, chances of success in a retest will be greatly improved.

SKATING INSTRUCTION

It is essential that a novice skater find a competent figure skating instructor or coach if real progress is to be made. Good coaches understand their pupils, and serve as teacher, disciplinarian, and friend. In return, the student must have complete confidence in the mentor.

A skater with competitive aspirations should not wait too long before joining forces with a coach. It's the best way to improve one's skills. For instance, a skater cannot see himself work on the ice, and a coach is the best person to point out and correct faults.

There is another member of your skating "team" that bears mention.

Lessons, equipment, and club fees cost money. Parents usually provide the financial support. A good skating parent (besides being willing to write checks) should be supportive in all areas of their child's skating development. Unfortunately, some skating parents, like stage mothers, can prove a hindrance to a child's skating progress. Their intentions are good, but an overbearing attitude can cause one to resent what one might otherwise enjoy. Try and develop a solid understanding with your parents as to your goals and desires. It will prove beneficial to both you and your folks.

OFF-ICE ACTIVITIES

I cannot place enough emphasis on the importance of off-ice activities to aid the competitive skater.

Ballet develops grace and beautiful arm movements, in addition to building a stronger back and body. This enables a skater to acquire increased limberness for spirals and split jumps.

Jazz and modern dance help a skater improve rhythm and timing. Many of the dance steps can be incorporated into routines used in show and exhibition skating.

Gymnastics is a good way to improve coordination. Even some of these moves can be adapted for use on ice.

Jogging and skipping rope increase stamina and lung capacity.

Weight lifting bolsters strength for pairs skaters.

The list goes on and on.

With all your efforts, the primary activity for anyone aspiring to become a real figure skater is to spend as much time as possible with boots laced and skates sharpened—skating, skating, skating.

Beginning Compulsory Figures

COMPULSORY FIGURES, also known as school figures, are the basis of figure skating.

Figure eights are the fundamental figures in the compulsories. They are formed by two, or sometimes three, circles skated from one starting point or center. The figure is divided in half lengthwise by an imaginary line, called a long axis.

All figures are usually skated on clean ice, so each line will be easy to see. It is most important that all figures be symmetrical, for the judging is based not only on your skating form, but also on the appearance of the print traced into the ice.

Strive to make all figures look like they have been drawn with a compass. An invention called a scribe, actually a huge compass, is used for scratching a perfect circle on the ice. The scribe is implemented to check the symmetry of a figure and points out uneven sections. Beginners will find this instrument a great aid when starting work on figures, as it helps skaters gain a feeling of making true circles.

The first test given by the United States Figure Skating Association to judge a skater's ability is the preliminary test. The test consists of the four edges, or rolls, skated on the ice on a long axis. After the basic rolls, outside and inside forward eights are skated. This is followed by the waltz eight.

OUTSIDE FORWARD EIGHT

This is the initial compulsory figure to learn.

Begin in the same position as outside edges. Stand in a

Shoulders and hips are along the short axis . . .

125

then push off on an outside edge to skate an outside forward eight . . .

as you cross the long axis, the free leg comes forward and the arm and shoulder position is reversed.

126

"T" position, right foot leading, with your back to the center of the right circle. Shoulders and hips should be along the short axis (the imaginary line that crosses the long axis at right angles through the joining point of the circles).

Push off as if to do a simple outside edge, but hold this position, with the free leg still, for the first half-circle. Make sure the skating knee is slightly bent.

As you cross the long axis (the halfway point), pass the free leg slowly forward and at the same time change the arms and shoulders. The legs and arms should pass so closely that they actually touch the body and other leg.

Make sure to point the toe of the free leg, but do not allow it to cross over the trace to the outside of the circle.

As you approach the center of the eight, bring the free foot in alongside the skate and bend the knees for the push-off into the left circle.

Turn the right foot out sideways a full 90° for the push and step.

The left skate must take the ice exactly on the initial starting point. A *very slight* open space will be acceptable.

Never allow your trace lines to cross.

When working on this move concentrate on this area of the circle, for the center of the eight is the most important segment when creating the figure.

INSIDE FORWARD EIGHT

The inside eight makes the same basic tracing as the outside eight, but with an opposite arm and hip position.

Begin in the "T" position, right foot leading and perpendicular to the long axis. Hips and shoulders should be parallel to the long axis. Lead with the left arm.

Push off, leaving the free leg inside the circle. Don't ever allow it to cross behind the skating leg. This will force you to swing around.

This position is held until the halfway point, where the arms reverse and the free leg passes forward.

It is important to remember *always* to point the toe of the free leg when it is in front.

As you close the circles, push off as before. Be sure the push is done with the whole blade turned out. Never implement a toe pick push.

One common fault is that the skater allows his body to lunge forward as he pushes off. Evenness is the key to success.

Circles on all eights should be skated with even speed. The diameter of the print should be approximately three times your height.

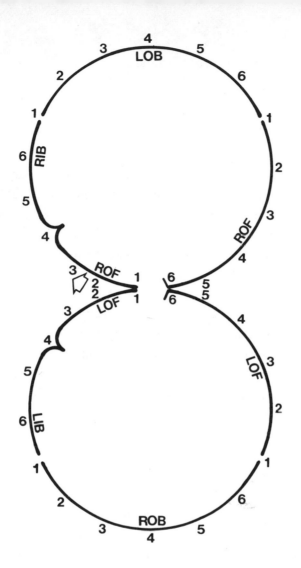

A diagram of the Waltz Eight, the final required maneuver on the Preliminary Test. From a push off (1–2–3); a right outside forward Three Turn (4); a right inside back edge (5–6); change to a left outside back edge and hold this (1–2–3) until crossing the long axis, then, turn to a left outside back edge (4–5–6) and push to a right outside forward edge and hold this for the next six counts.

WALTZ EIGHT

This is the final required move for the preliminary test.

The waltz eight is one figure eight with three segments; an outside forward push and outside three turn; a push or step to an outside back edge or roll; and finally a step and push to an outside forward roll.

This entire movement is then repeated in the other direction.

Each segment should cover exactly one-third of the circle, taking six counts per segment. Counting aloud as you perform the move may be helpful.

Start in a "T" position with the right foot leading.

Using the techniques previously learned, push off on 1–2–3; turn the right outside forward three turn on 4; and the right inside back edge on 5–6.

Push onto the left outside back edge with no head or arm movement.

Hold the next 1–2–3 across the top of the circle.

As you cross the long axis, turn into a left outside back position (looking over your left shoulder) on 4–5–6.

Let the body turn around to push forward into a right outside forward edge at the two-thirds point of the circle.

Hold this for the next six counts.

Do not change the arms or allow them to swing around as you pass the free leg forward.

All three turns should be practiced until they can

be done as cleanly as possible without scrapes. Clean turns, a certain amount of symmetry, and control are expected on the preliminary test.

Each figure is assigned a mark from one to six, with tenths of points to make an even finer evaluation.

The U.S.F.S.A. publishes *The Evaluation of Errors in School Figures*. This volume describes, in detail, each individual fault and the appropriate penalty for the error. Owning a copy of this book will prove invaluable for the test candidate or competitor.

The margin for error in school figures is slight. Major miscues can be made in the construction of the figure: creating uneven circle sizes, unrounded circles, or wobbly or widely traced circles.

Serious errors can be made in the turns. Turns must never be scraped or forced. The change of edge must take place along the long axis, or the print will clearly show a change of edge in the wrong place.

After passing the preliminary test it's time to prepare for the first regular test. From now on the tests become increasingly involved and difficult.

There are many new figures to be learned, and innumerable techniques to implement. What works for one skater may spell disaster for another. This is why it is most important to have a qualified instructor work with you on the more complex figures.

For reference, here is a list of some of the terms used in advanced figures:

Three Turn. This basic figure is cut in all tests from the

The print left by incorrect Three's. With a flat edge . . .

. . . with a change of edge in the wrong place.

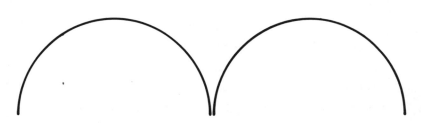

A Three Turn with an edge change at the top leaves an "open tip."

preliminary to the gold medal. It is done on any of the four edges and etches a deep number 3 in the ice. A clean turn is essential. A clean turn is one in which the change of edge takes place precisely at the midpoint of the turn. Making the actual point of the change of edge creates an open turn.

Change of Edge. This is used in most figures containing three circles, and in the paragraph figure. The edge changes when coming to the completion of a circle figure. At the exact point of the long axis the edge is changed and the skater continues along the line of the next circle.

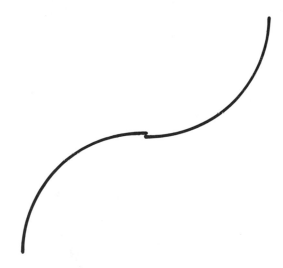

The print left by a change of edge.

Paragraph Figure. A most difficult figure in which both circles are skated on the same foot from the same initial thrust. This requires a powerful push-off to carry one through the turns to a change of edge at the center, with the movements repeated on the other side. This is the only figure in which six tracings appear on the ice because the figure is skated three times on each foot.

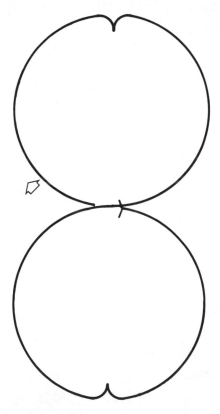

The Paragraph Three Turn is a most difficult figure to master.

Loop. This advanced figure is most difficult to master. It is a loop at the top of the circle. Skated on a much smaller circle than normal figures, its diameter is generally the height of the skater. Loops are done backward and forward, on inside and outside edges, with changes of edges, and as a paragraph figure.

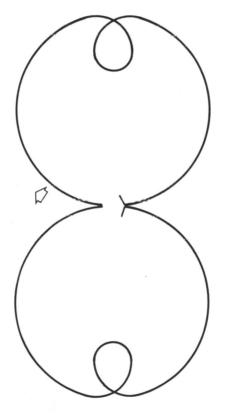

Loops are skated at the top of the circles.

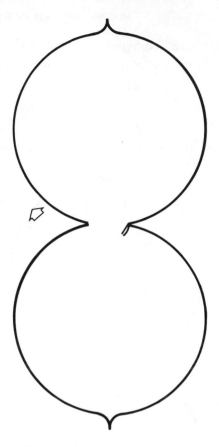

Diagram of the Bracket Turn.

Bracket. This is the opposite of the three turn. Instead of turning in toward the circle, the turn is pointed outside the circle. The change of edge still takes place exactly on the long axis, but instead of the tip being open it is slightly crossed. When perfectly skated, this is called a rabbit ear.

136

Counter. Similar to the bracket and three turn, the counter is done between two circles.

Rocker. The opposite of the counter. The skater turns toward the original circle.

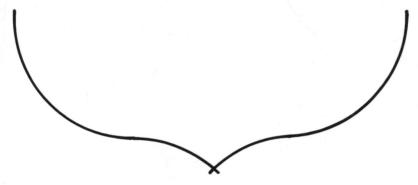

When skating a Bracket, the change of edge is made with the tip slightly crossed. The print created is known as "Rabbit Ears."

The pattern for the counter . . .

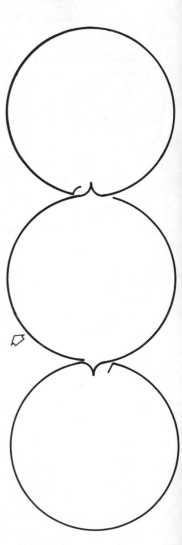

and its opposite move, the Rocker. In the Rocker you ska
towards the original circle.

Skating Competition

COMPETITIVE SKATING IS most exciting. You don't have to be an expert skater to enter competitions, as beginning skaters can join local clubs or organizations that sponsor events for all levels of skating skill. These competitions are an excellent way to gain on-ice confidence and personal satisfaction.

Over the many years I have been a competitive skater, I've found it beneficial to keep a journal. The journal makes it possible to chart progress and note which areas require additional work. Tips and tricks you've learned to correct specific errors should be included in your notations. This is a great asset when planning a day's skate. Refer to your notes, and relate them to your instructor's suggestions for a productive practice session.

Concentration is everything when skating figures in

competition or in tests. An inexperienced competitor may have difficulty keeping his mind from wandering, but the event need not be a nerve-shattering experience. It may ease your mind to know *all* the competitors are tense. The panel of judges may appear very stern and serious but their purpose is to evaluate your performance, not harm you.

Compulsory figures are the first work phase for a competitive skater. It will take many hours to perfect all the necessary fine points. When practicing, don't skate all your figures on a set line or path but lay them out as well. This means skating figures on clean ice, just as you will do in actual competition. Clean ice makes it easy to see where your faults are.

It is important to be able to line up a figure. As soon as you know which figures are to be skated, try and visualize how you will do them. Always measure the size of your circles during the warm-up period to get a better feel of your motion once the event begins. All circles should be equal in size along a straight axis.

Now it's time to take a deep breath and go out and do your best.

Before beginning, remember to indicate the long axis of your figure with both arms, and wait for the signal to start.

Make sure you have looked where you want to go prior to the push-off and know exactly where you want to etch that first trace. The initial trace should be round and symmetrical with all other prints equal to it.

If the first print is laid out correctly, the rest is easy. All you have to do is trace the circles (as well as possible) two more times. Finish the figure by stepping on the center line, at the intersection of the long and short axes, then glide straight out.

Now it's up to the judges. They will examine the figure, measure it, and check how cleanly the turns and edges have been done. Then they will assign their marks.

Free skating is a major aspect of skating competitions. The free skating program requires not only the ability to execute numerous ice movements, but the stamina to perform them almost effortlessly.

First the skating routine is created, orchestrating various jumps, spins, and other steps to music. The routine is practiced over and over until it all flows together as if it were a dance. Stamina can be developed by following a program rehearsal with a series of power strokes around the rink. Exerting yourself just a bit further than you think you can will aid in gaining strength.

Before donning skates, do some loosening-up exercises. Ballet exercises (knee bends, stretches, kicks, arm and body movements) will be very helpful in preparing the muscles and will make the skater feel more comfortable upon taking to the ice for a formal warm-up.

It's a good idea to practice your warm-up periods before actual competition time comes around. This accustoms the skater to a precompetition routine as well as the performance, which should make it even easier to lose

Deep knee bends are a valuable off-ice exercise.

Ballet pliés are excellent exercises to stretch leg muscles before taking to the ice.

This arabesque position aides in achieving better body extension.

those preskating jitters. If you have difficulty with a specific move during the warm-up, don't panic. You know you have practiced the move and are able to do it. Have confidence, it will work in the program.

A usual warm-up period lasts five minutes. This is a sufficient amount of time, so don't rush. Do some stroking to get the feel of the ice before going on to jumps and spins.

After the warm-up, clean your blades (place a towel on the rail near the entrance).

Know in advance when it will be your turn to skate. As

in the compulsory competition, use your warm-up time well. Then, when your name is called, take to the ice in a pleasing and confident manner.

Assume your starting pose and wait for the music to begin.

If you have practiced your program faithfully, every move will flow evenly into a well-skated program.

Enjoy yourself as you skate! Your pleasure will be contagious. The audience and judges will be more entertained by the routine if they feel they are sharing in your fun. When the routine has ended, take a bow and skate off the ice in good form.

After a contest, analyze your mistakes. Try to root out their sources. Welcome the judges' and coaches' constructive criticism. This can help identify and eliminate miscues and make the next performance even better.

Skating skills are necessary for competitive success, but do not discount the importance of a pleasant personal appearance.

Skates should be polished. The skating outfit must fit well, suit your skating style, and be appropriate for the skating event.

Hair should be well groomed. Females (and males) with long hair must be sure no pins can come loose during the routine. A hair pin on the ice can be a serious hazard to any skater.

Hairdos should not be so involved that they risk the possibility of becoming undone.

Competition is an exciting time. Skaters make new

friends and get the opportunity to view other skating styles. Careful observation may give you ideas to improve your own routine and overall performance the next time out.

Program
Construction

THE SEGMENT OF the figure skating competition consisting of continuous free skating done to music is known as a program, or routine. Competitions are won and lost during this segment of a contest. A well-constructed program is a great asset to an ambitious skater.

The length of a program depends upon the level of skating skill and the specific event entered. Programs run from two minutes up to a grueling five-minute performance. To skate for five minutes requires not only skating competence, but a great deal of stamina. It is necessary to be in top physical condition for a long routine.

Music is the first element to be chosen when planning a program. Selecting appropriate music is a must. Pick music you like. The music must become part of you and not just serve as background. There should be changes in tempo. In longer routines several pieces of music can be blended to serve this purpose. Exciting music is good while performing difficult jumps and steps. Slow, lyrical selections (waltzes, etc.) will complement steps and spins.

Once the musical decisions are made, a variety of dance steps, spirals, spins, and jumps should be planned to fit the music. Listen to the music several times before deciding on your maneuvers. Include only material you are capable of doing well. A program consisting of half-mastered moves will look terrible. Including one simple jump that is executed to perfection is going to do more for the program than fifty difficult steps that are not within your skating ability.

While practicing, if you find you are having difficulty with a specific move, drop it from the routine until it can be consistently carried out proficiently. A poorly executed jump or spin will ruin the harmonious composition of the routine, an important criterion in the judging.

The routine should be your own presentation, exhibiting your style and no one else's. You must feel comfortable and look well doing your chosen moves.

Even the simplest program must have a pattern. Be sure to include a strong opening and closing. This will provide a positive first and last impression for the audience and judges.

Use the entire ice during the program. Do not concentrate all jumps and spins in one area of the arena.

147

A routine must be rehearsed many times, reaching a point where it can be done without thinking. It is especially important in competition that the program and skater become one. Thinking of upcoming moves takes precious time away from "selling" the program. Use of physical and facial expressions to enhance the skating moves is a wise idea.

Even an experienced skater will need assistance in composing an effective program. A skater can "feel" the program, but not actually see the overall impression.

Once music and moves are chosen, get an honest opinion of your choices from a knowledgeable friend or coach. You've put so much time into construction of the program that it is difficult for you to be objective. It is not hard for a skater (even working with only one coach) to fall inadvertently into a pattern with little variety.

Training is an important part of any successful program. Even the best of routines will lose effectiveness when a skater starts out strong but lacks the conditioning to finish the program as forcefully as he began.

A good way to improve stamina is by practicing the program twice, back-to-back. It may seem impossible, but with serious work it becomes easier and easier. After the double routine has been skated, take a few quick laps around the rink. Finish the session by practicing some jumps. Not only will this type of training session build up leg muscles, it will also aid in gaining confidence that you can skate the program, with equal strength, from start to finish.

Physical conditioning will pay off in other ways. Skating in competition means working in a stress situation. Stress burns up energy. Without proper training, fatigue sets in sooner in these instances. Good conditioning helps combat stress fatigue.

Many skaters complement on-ice training with off-ice workouts. Jogging and jumping rope are excellent exercises. Endurance exercises increase lung capacity, which is a great asset as proper breathing is very important when skating a program. Your breathing should be deep. Never take short gulps of air or hold your breath. Always try to breathe naturally, as you do when asleep.

As you plan or practice a program, never lose sight of the elements the judges will consider important. They are interested in what you have chosen to perform, your ability to execute the moves, how you look while doing the routine, the flow from one move to another, and how these facets fit the music.

Ice Dancing

ICE DANCING made its debut as an Olympic event at the winter games of 1976. Raising the sport to this high plateau of competition brings it up the level of older forms of skating, and ice dancing is now recognized as a major area of figure skating.

Ice dancing is done with partners (mixed couples). The emphasis is on edges, steps, and skating, rather than the lifts and jumps of free or pairs skating.

In ice dancing on must initially learn the various positions, or holds.

HAND-IN-HAND

This is the easiest of the holds. Both partners skate side

by side and change hands to maneuver around each other.

WALTZ POSITION

This is also called the closed position, similar to a ballroom dancing position. The partners face each other while the female places her left hand against the male's shoulder. The male rests his right hand against her back at the shoulder blade. They clasp their free hands with the arms out to the side and with the elbows slightly bent.

KILLIAN POSITION

This is an open waltz position. Both partners skate in the same direction.

OPEN KILLIAN POSITION

A variation of the Killian. Partners stand side by side (the male on the left) and face in the same direction. The right hand of the male is placed on the female's right hip. She holds his hand with her right hand. Both skaters have their left arms extended to the side and slightly forward, holding hands.

These are the basic positions. As one progresses, more difficult dance holds will be learned.

Try these simple dance steps in tandem with your partner:

CROSS STEPS

These are easily mastered. Glide on one skate. Bring the free leg across the skating foot and let it glide alongside for a few counts. It then returns to the original position.

One variation is to allow the free leg to cross *behind* the skating foot.

CHASSE STEP

To skate a forward chasse, glide on the left foot with the right extended to the rear. Bring in the right foot alongside the left. Life the left foot slightly, gliding on the right foot for a few beats.

Place the left foot back on the ice and thrust into a new stroke with the right foot.

Practice this motion in time to music.

FORWARD PROGRESSIVE

This step is similar to the chasse. Begin on a left-foot

glide with the right extended behind.

Let the right foot come forward and lower it slightly ahead of, but still parallel to, the left foot.

Hold this position for a few beats. Then send the right skate back in a thrusting motion to gain speed on the left foot.

SLIDE CHASSE

The right foot is brought in as if a regular chasse were being skated. But after placing it beside the left, the left skate slides forward and off the ice, as weight shifts onto the right foot. It is important that as the leg comes off the ice it is straight and the toes are pointed.

All dance steps should be practiced while traveling backward as well as forward. Many steps and positions are combined to make up each dance.

Rinks have ice dancing clubs where instruction can be obtained. All the dances are listed and diagrammed in the U.S.F.S.A. rule book. Each dance has a specific pattern on the ice and is skated to a certain tempo. Although you can attempt to work from diagrams, formal instruction is advised.

Dance sessions at the rink provide the perfect opportunity to practice this form of skating. Dancers (singles and couples) line up at opposite sides of the rink and work on specific dances in a set pattern, at the same time. It is an excellent way to learn-by-doing.

Don't just barge in anyplace on the line and begin to follow along. Be sure you have enough space to work without interfering with the other skaters. Always skate in time to the music. Lack of courtesy will only detract from the pleasure of the session for all involved.

Ice dancing is divided into six tests, from the preliminary to the gold dance test.

Other dance competition categories are:

Original Set Pattern. In this category contestants skate to a specific rhythm. The skaters can choose any music of that rhythm and create their own steps and patterns. The routine is repeated three times.

Free Dancing. This category should not be confused with pairs skating. Free dancing is a program created by the dance team. The routine incorporates a variety of different steps, moods, and rhythms.

The category is carefully governed by a set of rules that define allowable and judgeable maneuvers. Although dance teams are not permitted to do the spectacular lifts, spins, and jumps that are seen in pairs skating, dancers awe the audience with their precision skating and interpretation of the music.

Pairs Skating

PAIRS SKATING differs from ice dancing in that it involves spins and jumps and a greater amount of free skating.

All basic jumps and spins are done in tandem. In addition, the couple executes an infinite number of lifts and spins. There are moves, such as the throw axel, in which the male partner actually throws the female member into a jump.

Pairs skating is a beautiful and exciting division of figure skating, but only experienced skaters should attempt its difficult maneuvers.

The first step in pairs skating is to find two skaters (one male, the other female) whose skating styles complement one another. This can be a difficult task. A graceful skater teamed with one with choppy stroking action is an

Kathy Normile and Greg Taylor of "Holiday On Ice" perform a high overhead lift.

awkward sight.

Brother and sister teams are often very successful as pairs partners. They seem to have an almost uncanny ability to achieve unison in their movements.

Don't despair if you lack a skating sibling. When two skaters team up and work long enough, and hard enough, they begin to think and skate as one, and this is the essence of successful pairs skating.

Glossary

Arabesque Position. A pose in which the skater glides on one leg while the other is extended high behind. Derived from the classical ballet position.

Arabian Cartwheel. Acrobatic jump similar to the off-ice gymnastic move.

Axel. An edge jump with a takeoff on a forward outside edge, 1½ revolutions in air, and a landing on a back outside edge. Same as waltz jump, with an extra revolution.

Back Spin. Spinning in the same rotation as any spin, only done on the other foot.

Backward Double Sculling. A method of gaining backward motion with both skates remaining in contract with the ice.

Ballet Jump. A simple toe jump that looks like an advanced maneuver.

Barrier. The railing around the edge of the ice.

Barrier Pull. A way for beginners to gain movement on the ice by pulling hand over hand along the barrier.

Blade. The part of the skate in contact with the ice. Made of highly tempered steel, it is sharpened periodically to fit the skater's need.

Blade guards. Made of rubber or wood, they slip over the blade to protect the steel. Should be worn when walking to and from the ice.

Boot. A specialized shoe of high-grade, strong leather, to which a skating blade is attached. Often custom fitted for the skater.

Bracket. An advanced figure. The bracket is a three turn turned inside out. The cusp points out of the circle instead of in.

Bunny Hop. The simplest jump to learn. A forward jump from the flat of one blade to the toe pick of the other, then back to the flat of the original takeoff skate. Done with no rotation.

Butterfly Cartwheel. See *Arabian Cartwheel.*

Camel Spin. A variation of the basic flatfooted spin, done in an arabesque position.

Center. The point of a figure where the long and short axes intersect.

Change of Edge. Switching from one edge to the other during a single glide.

Chasse Step. A basic ice dancing maneuver, in which the feet come together.

Checked Position. Finishing a move (spin, turn, etc.) with arms and upper body facing against the direction just turned.

Cherry Flip. Another term for toe loop.

Closed Position. See *Waltz Position.*

Compulsory Figures. The many variations of the basic figure eight. A very precise and exact art.

Counter. (1) The steel arch support built into the skate boot. (2) An advanced figure similar to the bracket and three turn. Done between two circles.

Cross Steps. A basic ice dancing maneuver in which one foot crosses the other's line of travel.

Crosscuts. The same as crossovers.

Crossovers. Strokes used to travel on a curve in which the feet cross over to step. Can be done forward or backward.

Double Axel. An edge jump with a takeoff from a forward outside edge, 2½ in-air revolutions, and a landing on a back outside edge.

Double Flatfooted Spin. A simple two-footed spinning maneuver.

Double Loop. An edge jump with a back outside takeoff, two revolutions in air, and a back outside landing.

Double Salchow. An edge jump with a back inside takeoff, two in-air revolutions and a back outside landing on the other foot.

Double Sculling. A method of skating which keeps both feet in contact with the ice with an in-and-out movement of the skates. A good exercise to develop inside edges and leg power.

Double Three. Two three turns in a row on the same foot and glide.

Edge Jump. A jump with a takeoff from one blade's running edge.

Edges. The two sides of each blade. These are identified as the inside and outside edge.

Euler Jump. See *Flip Jump.*

Figure Eight. (1) The fundamental figure in the compulsory figures. Formed by two, sometimes three, circles skated from one starting point. (2) A general term for all compulsory figures because they are skated in the shape of an eight.

Figure Skate. Skate designed especially for figure skating. The blade is slightly rounded with a toe pick at the front.

Flip Jump. A toe jump taken off from an inside back edge, with one in-air revolution and landed on the outside back edge of the other skate.

Flying Camel Spin. A back camel spin with a jumped entry.

Flying Sit Spin. A jumped entry sit spin. The landing is on the opposite foot from the takeoff.

Free Ankle. Ankle of the free foot.

Free Dancing. A dance competition category in which skaters select their own music and create their own program. The program will display a variety of steps, moods, and rhythms. Precision skating and interpretation of the music are important in this category.

Free Foot. The nonskating foot. Usually stretched with the toe pointed.

Free Hip. Hip on the side of the nonskating leg.

Free Knee. Knee of the nonskating leg. Used for power in jumps and spins.

Free Skating. Form of skating in which the skater is free to do whatever he wishes to do.

Forward Progressive Step. A basic ice dancing step. Similar to the chasse step.

Full Hockey Stop. Method of stopping with feet parallel to each other.

Glide. The actual motion of skating on ice.

Gold Dance Test. The highest level ice dancing test. See *Gold Medal.*

Gold Medal. The most complex figure skating test. Required moves are those seen in high-level skating competitions. Given in Figure, Ice Dance, and Pairs categories.

Graefstroem Spin. A low camel spin.

Jackson Haines. Creator of the modern concept of figure skating.

Half-Flip. Similar to a flip, but making only one-half a revolution, and coming out forward.

Half-Loop. An edge jump taken from a back outside edge, with one in-air turn and a back inside landing.

Hand-in-Hand. A basic ice dancing hold where the partners hold hands.

Sonja Henie. Innovator of modern artistic skating and creator of the ice show.

Hockey Skates. Used for ice hockey, where quick stops and changes of direction are needed. They have a much rounder blade than the figure skate.

Holds. The various positions used by ice dancers to hold on to each other.

Hollow. The space between the two edges on the blade.

Hooks. Located on the side of a boot. Are laced for support and can be adjusted for comfort.

Hops. Jumps without rotation.

Ice Dancing. A part of the figure skating sport in which partners skate together, to music, and incorporate a variety of edges, steps, general skating moves, and rhythms to create a program. Compulsory dances are much like ballroom dances, only done on ice. Tests in ice dancing range from the preliminary to the gold dance test. The sport made its debut as an Olympic event in 1976.

Ice Skating Institute of America. Association which governs a set of tests and competitions. Operates separately from the United States Figure Skating Association.

Inside Axel. An edge jump taken off from a forward inside edge, with one and a half revolutions and landed on a back outside edge.

Inside Backward Edge. A basic edge.

Inside Backward Roll. A basic roll. See *Rolls*.

Inside Edge. The edge on the inside of the skate, or leg, on a curve leaning into a circle.

Inside Forward Edge. A basic edge. The simplest to learn.

Inside Forward Eight. A compulsory figure required in the preliminary test.

Inside Forward Roll. A basic roll. See *Rolls*.

International Skating Union. (I.S.U.) The association that governs organized figure skating, speed skating, and hockey on an international level.

Journal. A record kept by a figure skater to chart progress, note helpful tips to correct skating erros, and remind one of areas for extra practice.

Jumps. A move in which the skater leaves the ice. Should not be attempted until edges and spirals have been mastered. There are many variations. Jumping is an important facet in the free skating routines.

Jump Sit Spin. A sit spin with a jumped entry, landing on the takeoff foot.

Killian Position. An ice dancing position. An open waltz position.

Long Axis Line. The line which bisects all the circles of a figure.

Loop. An advanced figure. A loop done inside at the top of the circle. Skated in a small circle, loops are done forward, backward, on inside or outside edges, with change of edge, or as a paragraph figure.

Lutz. A toe jump similar to the flip jump, except the takeoff is from an outside back edge. Named after its inventor.

Master Tooth. The large, oversized first toe pick on a figure skating blade. Used for jumping.

Mazurka Jump. A variation of the ballet jump.

Modified Hockey Stop. A method of stopping.

Modified T Position. A T position, in motion with a slight sideways angle.

Mohawk. The simplest forward to backward turn. The first basic turn to learn. The inside forward Mohawk is made from an inside forward edge on one foot to an inside back edge on the other skate. Outside Mohawks can be done, but are quite difficult.

One-Foot Axel. An edge jump taken off from a forward outside edge, with 1½ in-air revolutions and landing on a back inside edge on the takeoff foot.

One-Foot Eight. A figure eight in which both circles are skated from one initial thrust, remaining on that one foot.

Open Position. A variation of the Killian ice dancing hold.

Original Set Pattern. An ice dancing competition category. Contestants skate to a specified rhythm, selecting their own music of that rhythm. They create their own steps and pattern to fit the music.

Outside Backward Edge. A basic edge. Many jumps are landed on this edge.

Outside Backward Roll. A basic roll. See *Rolls.*

Outside Edge. The edge on the outside of a skate, or leg.

Outside Forward Edge. A basic edge.

Outside Forward Eight. A compulsory figure required in the preliminary test. The classic figure eight.

Outside Forward Roll. A basic roll. See *Rolls.*

Outside Forward Three Turn. The easiest one-foot turn. Used at the beginning of ice waltzes and many free skating maneuvers. An important part of school figures.

Pairs Skater. A skater who performs with a partner. The male is usually very strong, the female is lightweight and often petite.

Pairs Skating. A form of free skating. The two skaters incorporate lifts and spins, done together as well as seprately, into their routine.

Paragraph Figure. An advanced figure in which both circles are skated from an initial thrust. The only figure in which six tracings appear on the ice, as the figure is skated three times on each foot.

Pivot. A maneuver in which one skate toe is anchored in the ice as the body glides around it on the other foot's edge.

Preliminary Dance Test. The first ice skating test.

Preliminary Figure Test. The first figure skating test. Skaters are required to do the four basic rolls along a long axis, inside and outside forward eights, and a waltz eight. Prepares the skater for figure tests one through eight.

Print. The mark the blade makes on the ice.

Program. The segment of the figure skating competition consisting of free skating done to music. Also called a routine.

Richmond Trophy. A prestigious international competition for ladies (besides the World, Olympic, and European championships). Held annually just outside of London, in Richmond, England.

Rittenberger Jump. Another term for a loop jump.

Rocker. An advanced figure. Opposite of the counter. The skater now turns toward the original circle.

Rocker of a Blade. The degree of curve in the blade radius.

Rolls. Semicircles skated first on one foot, then the other, along the same axis. Done on outside forward, inside forward, outside backward, and inside backward edges. Rolls are the basis of school figures and free skating exercises. Rolls are required moves on the preliminary test.

Round Honed. A blade sharpened so it has two edges, with a hollow between.

Routine. See *Program.*

Run. Another term for crossovers or progressives.

Russian Split. A variation of the split jump. A sitting split is done with hands touching feet.

Salchow. The easiest of the edge jumps. Take off from a back inside edge, with one in-air turn and a landing on the back outside edge of the other foot.

School Figures. Compulsory figures.

Scribe. A compasslike device that traces a perfect circle on the ice. Used to check the symmetry of a skated figure.

Senior Lady Calssification. Usually the highest category in competition. Competitors are eligible upon passing the gold figure test.

Shadow Skating. Two people skating identical moves and stops as if one is the shadow.

Short Axis. The line dividing the two circles of a figure.

Single Flatfooted Spin. A spin done on the flat of one blade.

Single Forward Sculling. Similar to double sculling. One skate does the work as the other simply glides. Can be done on an alternate stroking basis.

Sit Spin. A variation of the basic flat spin. Done in a sitting position.

Skating Ankle. The ankle of the skating foot, which, depending on the lean and bend, determines the edge that is skated.

Skating Foot. The foot that is in contact with the ice.

Skating Hip. The hip of the skating leg, which, depending on the position, determines the steadiness and control of the skater.

Skating Knee. The knee of the skating leg. The skating knee should, ninety-nine percent of the time, have either a slight or deep knee bend.

Skidding Foot. Same as *Sliding Foot.*

Slide Chasse Step. A basic ice dancing step. A variation of the chasse step, in which the free leg slides forward.

Sliding Foot. The foot cutting the blade into the ice in a stopping maneuver.

Snow Plow. A method of stopping with toes turned in.

Speed Skate. A skate with a long, flat, thin blade to provide maximum pushing surface with a minimum of friction for obtaining great speeds on ice.

Speed Skating. Skating for speed, racing against other skaters or the clock. Done indoors on a short track, or outdoors— Olympic style.

Spins. Twirling on the ice. Must be done in one spot with a straight body position. Are done in numerous positions and from various edges. All figure skaters should try to become competent spinners.

Spiral. One of the most beautiful free skating moves. A glide done in an arabesque position.

166

Split Jump. An exciting toe jump that can be done by all levels of skaters. A hip-high split is done in midair.

Spread Eagle. A basic, and beautiful, figure skating maneuver. Done on two edges, fully turned out.

Stops. The method of deceleration accomplished by cutting the edge of a blade into the ice, creating friction to stop movement.

Stroking. The traditional skating motion which propels the skater forward or backward.

Swayback. A poor posture position. Leaning forward with stomach out and hips back.

Tap Jump. Same as *Toe Jump*.

The Evaluation of Errors in School Figures. A publication of the United States Figure Skating Association that describes faults and their corresponding penalties.

Three Jump. See *Waltz Jump*.

Three Turn. A turn done on one foot. Skated on either foot in either direction. The print, or design, on the ice is in the shape of the number three.

Throw Axel. A move done in pairs skating. The male member of the team actually throws the female partner into a jump.

Toe Jump. A jump with the takeoff point being the toe point of the free foot.

Toe Picks. The jagged edge at the front of a blade. Used for jumping and stopping.

Toe Push. A common error in figures. Using the toe point to push instead of the whole blade.

Toe Salchow Jump. Another term for a flip jump.

Toe Walley. Similar to a toe loop, but the takeoff edge is inside rather than outside.

Toeless Lutz. A lutz jump without the tap.

Tracing. Skating exactly over a previous mark or print.

Triple Loop. An edge jump with a back outside takeoff, three in-air turns, and a back outside landing on the same foot.

Triple Salchow. An edge jump taken off from a back inside edge with three revolutions in-air, and a back outside landing on the other foot.

T Position. A position from which to begin motion. One foot is placed in front, the other is placed at the instep perpendicular to the front skate.

T-Stop. A method of stopping in a T position.

United States Figure Skating Association (U.S.F.S.A.). The association that governs organized figure skating in the United States. Located in Boston, Massachusetts.

Walley. An edge jump from a back inside edge into one revolution and landed on a back outside edge. Similar to a loop, except for the back inside edge takeoff.

Waltz Eight. A compulsory figure required in the preliminary test. It is one figure eight done in three segments: outside forward push and outside three turn, push or step to an outside back edge or roll, and a step and push to an outside forward roll. This figure is then repeated in the opposite direction.

Waltz Jump. Also called a three jump. The first fundamental edge jump. The takeoff is from an outside forward edge, into a half revolution in-air, with the landing on the outside back edge of the other foot.

Waltz Position. Also called the closed position. An ice dancing hold. Similar to the position used in ballroom dancing.